TOP CRIMINAL CASES

THAT SHOCKED THE INDIA

SHRADDHA VERMA

TRUE SIGN
PUBLISHING HOUSE

Published by True Sign Publishing House
Address: SY. No. 21/2 & 21/3, Sonnenahalli,
Krishnarajapura, Bengaluru,
Karnataka - 560049 India
E-mail: truesignbooks@gmail.com
Website: www.truesign.in

Top Criminal Cases That Shocked The India
Author: Shraddha Verma

ISBN: 978-93-5584-970-0

First Edition: 2023

CONTENTS

Introduction

A crime is a deliberate act that causes physical or psychological harm, damage to or loss of property, and is against the law.

There are lots of different types of crime and nearly everyone will experience a crime at some point in their lives. Crime affects people from all backgrounds, locations and ages. In 2020–21, Victim Support staff and volunteers were in touch with 710,403 people affected by crime. We provided support to 153,100 victims of crime, 36% more than the previous year.

Criminal behaviour is defined by the laws of particular jurisdictions, and there are sometimes vast differences between and even within countries regarding what types of behaviour are prohibited. Conduct that is lawful in one country or jurisdiction may be criminal in another, and activity that amounts to a trivial infraction in one jurisdiction may constitute a serious crime elsewhere. Changing times and social attitudes may lead to changes in criminal law, so that behaviour that was once criminal may become lawful. For example, abortion, once prohibited except in the most unusual circumstances, is now lawful in many countries, as is homosexual behaviour in private between consenting adults in most Western countries, though it remains a serious offense in some parts of the world. Once criminal, suicide and attempted suicide have been removed from the scope of criminal law in some jurisdictions. Indeed, in the U.S. state of Oregon the Death with Dignity Act (passed in 1997) allows terminally ill individuals to end their lives through the use of lethal medications prescribed by a physician. Nonetheless, the general trend has been toward increasing the scope of criminal law rather than decreasing it, and it has been more common to find that statutes create new criminal offenses rather than abolishing existing ones. New technologies have given rise to new opportunities for their abuse, which has led to the creation of new legal restrictions. Just as the invention of the motor vehicle led to the development of a whole body of criminal laws designed to regulate its use, so the widening use of computers and especially the Internet has created the need to legislate against a variety of new abuses and frauds—or old frauds committed in new ways.

Tarakeswar Case, 1874

QUEEN VS NOBIN CHANDRA BANERJEE

INTRODUCTION

This case revolved around Murder and Adultery in the late 19th century. The murder by Nobin Chandra Bandopadhyay and adultery charges on the Mohanto of Tarakeshwar shrine. Unlike other cases of murder and adultery; this one caught the public eye and became a hot topic among the villagers and press. Newspapers covered the case right from the beginning and after the release of the accused, people also performed some plays related to the case of betrayal and adultery.

The Tarakeswar affair also known as Tarakeswar scandal or the Mahant-Elokeshi affair deals with public scandal in 19th century Bengal during the British Raj. It resulted from an illicit love affair between Elokeshi- the wife of government employee Nobin Chandra and the Brahmin head priest of the Tarakeswar Shiva temple. It was the assertion that Nobin slit his wife's head because of a love affair. The husband and the 'mahant' both were found guilty and the case highly publicized and covered almost every newspaper of 1873.

Society considered the mahant's actions as punishable and criminal, while justifying Nobin's action of killing an unchaste wife. The resulting public outrage forced authorities to release Nobin after two years. The scandal became the subject of Kalighat paintings and several popular Bengali plays, which often portrayed Nobin as a devoted husband. The mahant was generally presented as a womaniser, who took advantage of young women. The murder victim, Elokeshi, was sometimes blamed as a seductress and of being the root cause of the affair. In other plays, she was absolved of all guilt and was portrayed to have been tricked and raped by the mahant.

The tragedy is also represented in drawings and paintings. The people supported Nobin's killing of his wife and judged the move as a correct response to the adultery; that they believed his wife committed. But local arts and folk tales also suggest that; the Madhavchandra Giri, the *"powerful"* mahant of the popular and prosperous Tarakeswar temple, is the real evil person; who in the name of providing **fertility medication** to the Elokeshi, did the immoral act. An affair began with the *consent* of Elokeshi's parents. **(Though these are not proven facts but are prevalent equally in folk tales.)**

Elokeshi - The 16 years old housewife of the Bengali Government Employee.

ELOKESHI, the term of "Elokeshi" mean "women" with disheveled hair – A description for the ferocious Goddess of Destruction, Kali the protagonist of our story was also feared. Not for her strength to fight demons, but precisely on account of demons, that infected the minds of the people of that time – the fear of an independent woman with a mind of her own.

As a little girl in British- ruled Bengal, as in her life all the usual patterns were followed- like an early marriage to free the father of the burden of having an unmarried daughter, and then a long wait to grow up and be sought out by the husband.

Till then, Elokeshi was condemned to live in her village Kurmul in the 'safe' keep of her father Nilkamal Mukhopadhyay and step mother. Kurmul was only 70 kilometres away from Calcutta, the Queen Bee's Chamber in the honey comb of the Empire, which attracted people from far and wide.

Elokeshi had been wedded to a high caste Kulin Brahman, Nobin Chandra- the dream come true for any Bengalee father in those times. In fact, in the high tide of polygamy, many Kulin Brahmans made marrying young brides their occupation. They would criss- cross the Bengal countryside, going from village to village.

Elokeshi was the wife of the Bengali Government Employee Nobin Chandra Benerjee, she lived with her parents, in the village of Tarakeswar while Nobin was away for work in the Military Press in Calcutta.

Nobin Chandra – The Government Employee.

Nobin –an upper class Bengali who got a job in Military press,

It is rumored that when some kulins passed away, their pyres burnet for days as there would be a formidable line of brides in queue to commit Sati. Mercifully Nobin was not that kind. He loved his Elokeshi.

Yet, he thought it wise to leave his young bride in her father's care. Calcutta was no place for an uneducated village girl. She would be safer and better off away from the evils of the city, the young man thought. After all, whenever he could take leave, he would make it a point to go and visit his child bride.

Life was blessed. Nobin's only regret was that he desperately wanted a son, an heir. Elokeshi assured her husband that this was her wish too and that she had not spared any efforts. In fact, she had, in 1872, even reached out to a holy man to seek divine interdiction. The Holy Mahant, or priest of Taraknath Temple, Madhavchandra Giri had taken her under his protection and assured her that she would be blessed with a child soon.

Mahant or priest of Traknath Temple

Taraknath Temple

The mahant was generally presented as a womanizer, who took advantage of young women. The murder victim Elokeshi was sometimes blamed as a seductress and the root cause of the affair. In other plays, she was absolved of all guilt and was portrayed to have been tricked and raped by the mahant.

Mahant was a priest and he assured Elokeshi that she would beget a male child. That's why Elokeshi approached the Mahant of the popular and prosperous temple, seeking fertility medication, however the Mahant allegedly seduced and raped her. An affair began with the connivance of Elokeshi's parents.

The mahant was rumored to seduce women like Elokeshi who came to him for childbirth medicine and appropriate them with the help of his goons. After being raped, the women could not return to their family and languished in the brothels of Tarakeswar. In most plays, the mahant is described as drugging Elokeshi—by offering fake childbirth medicine—and then raping her. In the play Mohanter Dafarafa, a rare exception to the general theme of immorality in plays where the mahant misuses Elokeshi, his love is portrayed to be genuine and her seduction by him a resultant after-effect. However, later he is repentant.

On the day of incident – what happened ?

This is the story of the two scandalous trials that followed- which rocked the very foundations of the colonial government and a colonized people, and charted how the colonial judicial system would administer English justice to natives who were so taken by the novelty of the English legal system!

When Nobin returned to the village, he learned about the affair from village gossip. Nobin was publicly humiliated following the discovery of the affair. He confronted Elokeshi, who confessed and begged him for forgiveness. Not only did Nobin forgive her but he decided to run away with her from Tarakeswar. However, the mahant did not allow the couple to escape; his goons blocked their way.

On May 24, 1873, Nobin Chandra visited Elokeshi. Overcome with anger and jealousy, Nobin slit his wife's throat with a fish knife, decapitating her, on 27 May 1873. Full of remorse, Nobin surrendered to the local police station and confessed his crime.

"Hang me quick! This world is a wilderness to me. I am impatient to join my wife in the next". He was promptly produced before the Joint Magistrate of Sreerampur, who ordered him to hajat.

Nobin confessed his crime and it was later revealed that Elokeshi was having an affair with the Mohanto of the Tarakeshwar temple, Madhabchandra Giri. Nobin and the Mohanto both were represented before the court and were alleged with Murder and Adultery respectively.

Trial before the Court

The Tarakeswar murder case of 1873 (Queen vs Nobin Chandra Banerjee first stood in the Hoogly Sessions Court at Sera pore in south-west Bengal. The Indian jury acquitted Nobin, accepting his plea of insanity.

The decision of the Hoogly Court came after Woomesh Chandra Bonnerjee defended Nobin with the logic; that Nobin's act was merely an act in insanity and that he was not in control of himself; when he got to know about his wife's affair. Bonnerjee tried to prove Nobin's action was a result of temporary insanity; and he had no control over what he was saying or doing. The court agreed to the logic and held Nobin 'not guilty'

but the British judge Field overruled the jury's decision and forwarded the matter to the Calcutta High Court. However, Judge Field accepted that there was an adulterous relationship between Elokeshi and the mahant, with whom she was seen "joking and flirting".[Judge Markby, who presided over the case in the High Court, also accepted the evidence proving adultery.. The High Court convicted both Nobin and the mahant. Nobin was sentenced to life imprisonment; the mahant got 3 years rigorous imprisonment and a fine of ₹2000.

TRIAL-1

- Whether Nobin was insane or not?

- Whether Nobin was clearly of unsound mind while committing the act or not?

TRIAL-2

- Whether Nobin and Elokeshi were married and was it a known fact or not?

- Did Nobin knew about the affair and accepted the same or not?

- Whether there was sufficient proof or evidence to tell that sexual intercourse had occurred between the defendant and Elokeshi or not?

- Whether the defendant knew that his mistress was married or not?

For TRIAL-1

- If Nobin is proved of unsound mind at the time of committing the act; then he would be held not guilty of the murder of his wife Elokeshi.

For TRIAL-2

- If the marriage between Nobin and Elokeshi is not proved then the defendant would not be liable for adultery.

- Even afterwards, if Nobin knowingly about the affair and accepted the same of his wife and defendant; then the defendant could not be charged with Adultery.

- If sexual intercourse had not taken place between Nobin's wife and the defendant; then also the defendant could not be charged with Adultery.

- If the defendant was unaware of the fact that Elookeshi was already married then the defendant did no wrong of Adultery; as he was acting with a Bonafide intention.

TRIAL-1

The High Court held that there was no doubt that Elokeshi was killed with a **boti** (a Kitchen Knife) by the defendant of which the defendant himself confessed. For the question of the unsoundness of mind of the defendant, while committing the act; the court held that the defendant had been excited but not insane while slitting his wife's throat. The defendant acted under the influence of **'anger, jealousy, and grief'**; but had the sense that what he was doing was wrong.

The court declared the defendant sane and guilty of culpable homicide. The Court added that there is no sufficient evidence; that proved the defendant insane and unable to know the consequences of his act. Therefore, the court quashed the decision of the Hoogly Court; and sentenced the defendant under Section 302 of the Penal Code to transportation for life.

TRIAL-2

The High Court after the relevant arguments and proofs upheld the decision of the Subordinate Court; and sentenced the defendant **(Mohanto)** with 3 years of imprisonment and Rs.2000 of fine.

The court explained that it is adhering to the Hindu Law rites; and defending Hindu Law as Adultery was a criminal offense in British India. It was also noted that for the proof that the carnal intercourse took place between the defendant and Nobin's Wife; the court accepted the testimony of three residents; who confirmed that they saw Elokeshi entering into the defendant's house in the evening and returning in the morning.

The court accepted the testimony though they were weak proof; and also quoted the lines of Manu **"a woman must never act independently of her husband."** and stated that a woman could not visit a religious festival or holy place alone. Finally, the court stated that they place the law above personal revenge and individual justice.

PUBLIC REACTION

The newspaper Bengalee remarked: "People flock to the Sessions Court as they would flock to the Lewis Theatre to watch Othello being performed". The courtroom drama became a public spectacle. Authorities had to charge an entrance fee to control the crowds at the Hoogly Sessions Court. The right of admission was also restricted to those literate in English, citing that the mahant's British lawyer and the judge only spoke in English.

The overruling of the Indian jury's decision by the Sessions Court judge was heavily debated. According to Swati Chattopadhyay (author of Representing Calcutta: Modernity, Nationalism and the Colonial Uncanny), the court proceedings were seen as an interference by the British in local matters. The court represented a conflict between village and city, the priest and bhadralok (Bengali gentleman class) and the colonial state and nationalist subjects. The court proceedings were disturbed several times by crowds demanding clemency for Nobin or stringency for the mahant. The mahant and his English lawyer were often attacked outside the court. The mahant's punishment was termed lenient by the Bengali public. Nobin was released in 1875, following several public petitions for pardon. Such pleas came from members of the Calcutta elite and district town notables, local royals and "acknowledged leaders of native society", as well as from the "lower middle class"—from whom a 10,000-signature mercy plea was received.

Assessment and portrayal of the characters

Most accounts agree that Nobin loved his wife dearly, evidenced by the fact that he was ready to accept his wife at first and run away with her, even after knowledge of the affair. In an era where the chastity of a wife was highly valued, Nobin's blind love and acceptance of a guilty wife were deemed inappropriate by a large section of society. Her murder was considered justifiable. Some songs criticize Nobin's stupidity of trying to save his adulterous wife and thereby risking his own life. Police reports, confirming Nobin's love, read that after the murder, Nobin rushed to the police saying: "Hang me quick. This world is wilderness to me. I am impatient to join my wife in the next [world/life]", a line reported verbatim in newspapers as well as used in plays and songs. Some public petitions argued that given a choice to leave Elokeshi in the arms of the mahant to live a life of dishonour—which was worse than death—and to kill her, like a true husband, Nobin chose the latter to end her misery. However, some plays portray that Nobin has a mistress in town so leaves his wife in the village.

THE MAHANT OFFERS ELOKESHI CHILDBIRTH MEDICINE, TO DRUG HER BEFORE RAPING HER

Most of the plays were named to suggest the main crime was not Elokeshi's murder by Nobin, but the immoral activities of the mahant. The mahant is portrayed as the root cause of Elokeshi's death, which was an "inevitable conclusion" of the mahant 's activities. Elokeshi, "the object of desire", had to be killed by Nobin to restore his honour. Titles of such plays reinforce the theme and focus on the mahant's crime. Examples include: Mohanter Chakrabhraman, Mohanter Ki Saja, Mohanter

Elokeshi is sometimes depicted as a courtesan, indicating that she is the one who seduces the mahant. She is often described as unchaste and to have developed the adulterous affair and even lived with him for some time despite the fact that he first rapes her. The prostitutes empathize with Elokeshi, another victim of male lust and lament her fall from grace, which for them illustrates the fragile status of a wife.

The Murder Of Ghosts 1959

INTRODUCTION

This is a historic case where the people used to believe in the existence of the supernatural powers. In this case, an incident happened where the accused took the defense on the basis of existence of supernatural beings like ghosts. The court here tried whether the defense was valid or not.

The defense of wrong facts used in the cases may vary to certain extent depending on the facts of that case. The duty of the law is to ensure that the defense of mistake of facts is not misused or justice is not denied to the victims. This can be done by ensuring certain standards or principles which can apply to all cases universally.

The court is in a place where it has to observe that the accused did act in good faith which is defined under section 52 of IPC and also ascertain the fact that he did not have any injurious intention while he was attacking the person, in addition to it, the accused must also have acted with due care and attention. Understanding the term 'good faith' is not only used to determine the mental state of the accused but also for the reasonableness of the offence and it has to be a relevant consideration in allowing the defense.

Rasgovindpur – the Village of ghosts

In a village named Rasgovindpur in the Balasore district of Orissa, an aerodrome was abandoned. There was a lot of valuable scrap in the aerodrome and so, the Garrison Engineer of the Defence Department kept the aero scrap in charge of two chowkidars, namely Dibakar and Govind, to prevent the theft of the scrap. One Jagat Bandhu of Chatterji Brothers, Calcutta came to Rasgovindpur accompanied by a Nepali servant named Ram Bahadur Thapa to purchase the scrap sometime in April 1958. They were staying at the house of one Krishna Chandra Patro who was a tea stall owner in the area. Adivasis comprising of Santhals and Majhis resided in the nearby villages of the aerodrome and it was believed that ghosts lived in the aerodrome. As most of the footpaths to villages cut across the aerodrome, the Adivasis preferred not to go out alone at night along these paths.

Jagat Bandhu chatterji and Ram Bahadur Thapa ;---Curiosity to see ghost- how they planned to see them.

On 20th May, 1958 one Chandra Majhi who resided in the village Telkundi went to Krishna Chandra Patro's tea stall at 9 p.m. and fearing the ghosts decided to seek shelter at the tea stall for the night Despite the notoriety the place had attained and the fear spread among the people, Jagat Bandhu Chatterji and his servant, Ram Bahadur Thapa were eager to see the ghosts. So, they persuaded Krishna Chandra Patro to accompany them.

Day of incident

The three men escorted Chandra Majhi to his village Telkundi and then started walking through a footpath across the aerodrome to reach Rasgovindpur. While they were passing through Camp No. IV, they noticed a flickering light at a distance of 400 cubits along the pathway. The blowing wind and the movement of lights created an impression that it was not a natural light but a 'will-o the wisp'. There were also some apparitions seen in the light and the party suspected that the ghosts were dancing in the light and rushed to the place. The Nepali servant reached the spot first and started attacking the figures indiscriminately with a 'khurki'. Krishna Chandra Patro reached the spot sometime later and was mistakenly attacked by the servant (respondent) with a massive blow of the khurki. Krishna Chandra Patro cried in agony and started shouting that the Nepali had hit him. In the meantime, the rest of the figures also started crying in pain and the respondent put a stop to his actions. It was later discovered that the figures attacked by the respondent were not ghosts but the local Majhi women who had gathered around a 'mohua tree' at that hour of night to collect 'mohua' flowers with the help of a hurricane lantern. Resulting from the indiscriminate attacks of Ram Bahadur Thapa, one Gelhi Majhiani was killed and two women, named Ganga Majhiani and Saunri Majhiani were grievously injured. Krishna Chandra Patro was also grievously hurt.

SECTION UNDER THEY WERE CHARGED

The respondent was charged under Section 302 of the Indian Penal Code (IPC) for the murder of Gelhi Majhiani and under Section 326 of Indian Penal Code for injuring Ganga Majhiani and Saunri Majhiani and also under Section -324 of Indian Penal Code for causing hurt to Krishna Chandra Patro.

Trial in court

The Session court acquitted the accused servant on the reasoning that he was protected under Section 79 of Indian Penal Code based on the facts and circumstances of the case.

ISSUES RAISED

The issue raised before the honourable High Court was whether the killing and injuring people by the accused could be held reasonable under Section 79 of the Indian Penal Code (IPC)

provided that;- it was a mistake committed by him and whether the act could be considered in good faith as in Section 52 of IPC. The other issue raised was that whether a little extra care and attention would have averted the following incident. RULE APPLIED CASE ANALYSIS While discussing that under Section 79 of Indian Penal Code a crime committed under good faith and the person believing that he was justified in his/her act and Section 52 of IPC stating that good faith requires due attention .

The conduct of the person who is in question is determined on the basis of the intelligence and capacity of the person. It is only to be expected that the honest conclusions drawn by a mind of a calm and philosophical person would differ from the conclusions drawn by a mind of sectarian zealot and untrained to the habits of reasoning. That the law does not expect all persons to take due care and attention regardless of the positions they hold. The question of good faith should be considered according to the facts and circumstances of the case. Nevertheless, the High Court ruled that the accused would be protected under Section 79 of Indian Penal Code because the circumstances under which the apparition appeared before him and pre-disposition, it would be reasonably believed that the accused believed in good faith that there were ghosts present at the spot.

ANALYSIS OF JUDGEMENT

The court considered that it was fairly contended that the attack made by the accused servant was due to the fact of his belief that there were ghosts present at the spot and he did not have even a slight knowledge that the figures seen from a distance were that of human beings and not ghosts as inferred by him. The court thoroughly analyzed the facts of the case and interpreted the entire scene through the two witnesses, Krishna Chandra Patro and Jagat Bandhu Chatterji. After thoroughly analyzing the statements of the witnesses, the court held that there were inconsistencies with the statements of Krishna Chandra Patro who had materially contradicted his own statement under Section 164 of the Indian Penal Code (IPC).

Krishna Chandra Patro previous statement under Section 164

He had stated that he was forced by the "Bengali Babu", i.e., Jagat Bandhu Chatterjee to go out to see the ghosts. But, in the court of the Sessions Judge, he had given the statement of not admitting the above but that he hadgone out with Jagat Bandhu Chatterjee at midnight to see the ghosts.

The court stated that although Jagat Bandhu Chatterjee was the master of the accused but there was no sympathy shown by him towards the accused and he had been very consistent in his statements. So, the court felt it better to consider Jagat Bandhu's statementsover Krishna Chandra Patro's statement. Also, even Chandra Majhi who had earlier given the statement to the police that he had taken shelter at the tea stall for the night as he was afraid to go back to his village due to his fear of ghosts and had agreed only at the assurance by the accused servant, master of the accused servant and Krishna Chandra Patro that they would escort him back to his village and then reverted from his statement in the Sessions court by stating that he was not afraid of ghosts and was a brave man. So, the court decided not to givetoo much importance to his evidence .

Jagat Bandhu Chatterjee's statement

Jagat Bandhu Chatterjee's statement was that he and the accused servant were new to the area and had come just for business purposes and had been there just six months before the incident. The aerodrome was known to be infested with ghosts and it was believed that the ghosts used to move about in open fields on Tuesdays and Saturdays alternately. The night the incident took place was a Tuesday and the witness himself and the accused servant were anxious to view the ghosts and therefore they induced Krishna Chandra Patro and Chandra Majhi to accompany them to the spot. He also confirmed the fact that Chandra Majhi had stayed at the tea stall for the night due to his fear of ghosts. The whole party was excited to view the ghosts and they believed that owing to the day and the time, the ghosts could be easily viewed at the aerodrome. After dropping

Chandra Majhi at his village, Telkundi, the party on returning, saw the lights and the figures to which Krishna Chandra Patro shouted "Here are the ghosts". Thereupon the servant without waiting for a second, rushed to the place through the shortest path and started attacking the figures indiscriminately with his khurki believing them to be ghosts.

Krishna Chandra Patro followed the regular path instead of the shorter one and when mistakenly attacked by the accused servant, shouted. Only after the shouting of Krishna Chandra Patro did the accused servant come back to his senses. The master also testified that the accused servant was a firm believer of ghosts and that his actions were based on his belief that he was attacking ghosts and not human beings.

Court point of view

The court stated that the benefit of Section 79 of Indian Penal Code is given to a person who committed an act by mistake but his intentions were good. The good faith of an act can be deduced by the facts and circumstances of the case. The court also took notice of Section 52 of the Indian Penal Code (IPC) which states that the good faith in committing an act requires due care and attention and stated that there is no common standard available to determine the valid attention and care and it depends on case to case basis. The circumstances and facts of the case determine whether the attention and care taken by the accused were adequate or not. The court analyzed the facts of the case and summed them up in the favour of the accused servant by stating as follows –

The accused servant was new to the place and had only heard of the presence of the ghosts at the aerodrome. Moreover, the news that the ghosts were present there on Tuesdays and Saturdays and the fact that the night of the incident was a Tuesday, the accused's master and Krishna Chandra Patro's accompanying him and no one making any efforts to remove the impression of ghosts from the accused's mind, Krishna Chandra Patro's yelling that the ghosts were present at the spot and the lights and the movement of figures made the accused servant confident in his belief that there were ghosts present at the spot. So, the court stated that the benefit of Section 79 of Indian Penal Code is given to a person who committed an act by mistake but his intentions were good. The good faith of an act can be deduced by the facts and circumstances of the case.

The court also took notice of Section 52 of the Indian Penal Code (IPC) which states that the good faith in committing an act requires due care and attention and stated that there is no general standard available to determine the valid attention and care and it depends on case to case. The circumstances and facts of the case determine whether the attention and care taken by the accused were adequate or not. The court analyzed the facts of the case and summed them up in the favour of the accused servant by stating as follows – The accused servant was new to the place and had only heard of the presence of the ghosts at the aerodrome. Moreover, the news that the ghosts were present there on Tuesdays and Saturdays and the fact that the night of the incident was a Tuesday, the accused's master and Krishna Chandra Patro's accompanying him and no one making any efforts to remove the impression of ghosts from the accused's mind, Krishna Chandra Patro's yelling that the ghosts were present at the spot and the lights and the movement of figures made the accused servant confident in his belief that there were ghosts present at the spot. So, depending on these facts it would be irrelevant to deduce that the servant would have paused on the indication and taken time to reason whether the figures present were ghosts or human beings. His immediate reaction was to rush to the incident spot and attack the ghosts. Although evidence given by Dibakar and Govind, the chowkidars of the aerodrome, showed that the accused had a torch with him and argued that the accused could have used the torch to verify the presence of humans. However, the court felt that there was no reason for the accused to have any doubt regarding the presence of the ghosts as the local facts regarding the ghosts and no intervention made by the other two companions to enlighten him about the wrong impression but confirming to his thoughts through their actions and the accused's own belief in ghosts made his thoughts even more firm about the presence of ghosts at the aerodrome. The court held that the accused servant was protected under Section 79 of the Indian Penal Code (IPC)

Hammersmith Ghost Murder Case 1804

INTRODUCTION

The **Hammersmith Ghost murder case** of 1804 set a legal precedent in the UK regarding self-defence: that someone could be held liable for their actions even if they were the consequence of a mistaken belief.

Near the end of 1803, many people claimed to have seen or even been attacked by a ghost in the Hammersmith area of London, a ghost believed by locals to be the spirit of a suicide victim. On 3 January 1804, a 29-year-old excise officer named Francis Smith, a member of one of the armed patrols set up in the wake of the reports, shot and killed a bricklayer, Thomas Millwood, mistaking the white clothes of Millwood's trade for a shroud of a ghostly apparition. Smith was found guilty of murder and sentenced to death, later commuted to one year's hard labour.

The issues surrounding the case were not settled for 180 years, until a Court of Appeal decision in 1984.

Ghost

From November 1803, a number of people in the Hammersmith area claimed to have seen, and some to have been attacked by a ghost local, people said the ghost was of a man who had committed suicide the previous year and had been buried in Hammersmith churchyard. The contemporary belief was that suicide victims should not be buried in consecrated ground, as their souls would not then be at rest. The apparition was described as being very tall and dressed in all white, but was also said to wear a calfskin garment with horns and large glass eyes at other times.

Stories about the ghost soon began to circulate. Two women, one elderly and the other pregnant, were reported to have been seized by the ghost on separate occasions while walking near the churchyard; they were apparently so frightened that they both died from shock a few days afterwards. A brewer's servant, Thomas Groom, later testified that, while walking through the churchyard with a companion one night, close to 9:00 pm, something rose from behind a tombstone and seized him by the throat. Hearing the scuffle, his companion turned around, at which the ghost "gave me a twist round, and I saw nothing; I gave a bit of a push out with my fist, and felt something soft, like a great coat."

On 29 December, William Girdler, a night watchman, saw the ghost while near Beaver Lane and gave chase; the apparition threw off its shroud and managed to escape. With London not having an organized police force at the time, and as "many people were very much frightened," according to Girdler, several citizens formed armed patrols in the hope of apprehending the ghost.

DAY OF INCIDENT – MURDER OF THOMAS MILLWOOD

At the corner of Beaver Lane, while making his rounds at around 10:30 pm on 3 January 1804, Girdler met one of the armed citizens patrolling the area, 29-year-old excise officer Francis Smith. Armed with a shotgun, Smith told Girdler he was going to look for the supposed ghost. Girdler agreed that he would join Smith after he had called the hour at 11:00 pm, and that they would "take [the ghost] if possible." They then went their separate ways.

Just after 11:00 pm, Smith encountered Thomas Millwood, a bricklayer who was wearing the normal white clothing of his trade: 'Linen trousers entirely white, washed very clean, a waistcoat of flannel, apparently new, very white, and an apron, which he wore round himself'. Millwood had been heading home from a visit to his parents and sister, who lived in Black Lion Lane. According to Anne Millwood, the bricklayer's sister, immediately after seeing her brother off, she heard Smith challenge him, saying "Damn you; who are you and what are you? Damn you, I'll shoot you", after which Smith shot him in the left of the lower jaw and killed him.

After hearing the shot, Girdler and Smith's neighbour, one John Locke, together with a George Stowe, met Smith, who 'appeared very much agitated'; upon seeing Millwood's body, the others advised Smith to return home. Meanwhile, a constable arrived at the scene and took Smith into custody. Millwood's corpse was carried to an inn, where a surgeon, Mr. Flower, examined the body on 6 January and pronounced death to be the result of "a gunshot wound on the left side of the lower jaw with small shot, about size No. 4, one of which had penetrated the vertebra [sic] of the neck, and injured the spinal marrow.

Trial of Francis Smith

Smith was tried for willful murder. The deceased's wife, Mrs. Fulbrooke, stated that she had warned him to cover his white clothing with a greatcoat, as he had already been mistaken for the ghost on a previous occasion.

On Saturday evening, he and I were at home, for he lived with me; he said he had frightened two ladies and a gentleman who were coming along the terrace in a carriage, for that the man said, he dared to say 'there goes the ghost'; that he said he was no more a ghost than he was, and asked him, using a bad word, did he want a punch of the head; I begged of him to change his dress; Thomas, says I, as there is a piece of work about the ghost, and your clothes [sic] look white, pray do put on your great coat, that you may not run any danger;

— MRS. FULBROOKE'S WIFE OF THOMAS TESTIMONY AT THE OLD BAILEY TRIAL

Millwood's sister testified that although Smith had called on her brother to stop or he would shoot, Smith fired the gun almost immediately. Despite a number of declarations of Smith's good character, the chief judge, Lord Chief Baron Sir Archibald Macdonald, advised the jury that malice was not required of murder – merely an intent to kill:-

I should betray my duty, and injure the public security, if I did not persist in asserting that this is a clear case of murder, if the facts be proved to your satisfaction. All killing whatever amounts to murder, unless justified by the law, or in self-defence. In cases of some involuntary acts, or some sufficiently violent provocation, it becomes manslaughter. Not one of these circumstances occur here.

— Lord Chief Baron Macdonald

The Lord Chief Baron observed that Smith had neither acted in self-defense nor shot Millwood by accident; he had not been provoked by the supposed apparition nor had he attempted to apprehend it. Millwood had not committed any offence to justify being shot, and even if the supposed ghost had been shot, it would not have been acceptable, as frightening people while pretending to be a ghost was not a serious felony, but a far less serious misdemeanour, meriting only a small fine.

The judge closed his remarks by reminding the jury that the previous good character of the accused meant nothing in this case. Macdonald directed the jury to find the accused guilty of murder if they believed the facts presented by the witnesses. After considering for an hour, the jury returned a verdict of manslaughter. Macdonald informed the jury that "the Court could not receive such a verdict", and that they must either find Smith guilty of murder, or acquit him; that Smith believed Millwood was a ghost was irrelevant. The jury then returned with a verdict of guilty. After passing the customary sentence of death, Macdonald said that he intended to report the case to the King, who had the power to commute the sentence. The initial sentence of hanging and dissection was commuted to a year's hard labour.

The huge publicity given to the case persuaded the true culprit to come forward: John Graham, an elderly shoemaker, had been pretending to be a ghost by using a white sheet to frighten his apprentice, who had been scaring Graham's children with ghost stories. There is no record of Graham ever being punished.

—*Lord Chief Justice Lane*

The appeal was allowed, and the conviction quashed. The decision was approved by the Privy Council in and was later written into law in the Criminal Justice and Immigration Act 2008, Section 76.

The Tandoor Murder Case 1995

INTRODUCTION

What happens when you find your beloved partner engaged in a deep telephonic conversation with a person of opposite sex? You choose to shoot your partner in a fit of rage, chop the body into pieces, and to destroy the evidence you go ahead and burn the entire corpse in a "Tandoor". This is what happened exactly in the case of Sushil Sharma and Naina Sahni.

Naina Sahni was the victim of the tandoor murder case. On 2 July 1995, she was killed by her husband Sushil Sharma, a Congress youth leader and Member of the Legislative Assembly. Naina herself was a worker in the congress party. Sushil Sharma was convicted for the murder by the Trial Court, Delhi High Court and Supreme Court. On 8 December 2020, Sharma was not found guilty by the High Court.

NAINA SAHNI – THE VICTIM

Naina Sahni (the deceased) also a Delhi University Graduate, was the former General Secretary of the Delhi Youth Congress Girls Wing. It was said that Naina Sahni used to visit accused Sushil Sharma at the office of Youth Congress in New Delhi.

In the year 1992, accused Sushil Sharma obtained a flat at Mandir Marg where Naina Sahni used to visit frequently and at times "she used to stay back at night as well", as said by the neighbors. Later, Sushil and Naina are said to have married in that residence "in their own way", which suggests that they had a secret marriage hidden from the public; however, the marriage had the consent of both the parties, Sushil and Naina, also including Naina Sahni's parents. Thereafter, Naina continued to live in the said flat, claiming to be Sushil's wife, till she was murdered.

She is contemplating a future far away, and there is no place for her husband in her plans. Intelligent, ambitious and strikingly attractive, Naina has managed to graduate from university, obtain a pilot's licence and hold a position in the Congress party.

Lifestyle of Naina Sahni

Delhi is steaming. Those who can afford to, take shelter behind desert air coolers which, while a boon in the scorching dry heat of April and May, offer less relief in the sultry months of July and August.

Still, the whirring of cooler fans in apartment windows – complemented by the distant rumbling of traffic and punctuated by the odd raucous dialogue from behind closed doors – is the soundtrack of this Sunday evening in Mandir Marg. The streets are all but deserted; everyone is going about their lives, finishing the day's chores, making dinner or simply relaxing with the only affordable pastime in those days – television.

Day before the incident

At about seven in the evening, Naina dials Jagdish Taneja at the video library in the neighbourhood and asks him to deliver two cassettes. She then rings up her confidant and former lover, Matloob Karim, at his residence. She asks him whether he has visited Ram Swaroop, the travel consultant in Jor Bagh, to collect her visa for Australia. Matloob tells her he will in a day or two, and with that they end the conversation.

Naina's live-in partner, paramour, lover and unofficial husband Sushil Sharma drives into the apartment complex at around 8.15pm, parks his car and lets himself into the apartment. There is no loving welcome from Naina, but she quietly offers him a drink. The simmering tension between the two is palpable, even as Sushil pours the drink and both partake in their favourite tipple. There isn't much exchange of conversation – not for the moment, anyway.

SUSHIL SHARMA – CONGRESS YOUTH POLITICIAN

Sushil is the unofficial husband of the Naina Sahni. Starting with the background, Sushil Sharma was the President of Delhi Youth Congress at the relevant time (1992), a commerce graduate from Delhi University.

For some time now, he has doubted Naina's fidelity, and he may have reason for doing so. The consummate politician that he is, he senses keenly the changed tenor of their relationship, and he can feel her drawing away from him. That his political fortunes have recently ebbed is also gnawing at him. While the fact that he has forsaken her by refusing to acknowledge their relationship publicly eludes him, Sushil is roiling inside that his Naina is forsaking him just when he needs her support the most.

He is stung, too, by her displays of arrogance and rebelliousness, which have become all too frequent of late. A couple of months ago, she had raised her hand at him, and he still dwells grimly on it, his mind dark and clouded with jealousy. As their relationship has deteriorated, he has maintained surveillance on her. Whether real or imagined, Sushil sees signs of Naina's betrayal everywhere.

On the day of incident

The next day , Pradeep Sharma, the video shop attendant, arrives and delivers the two cassettes. Pradeep sees Naina and Sushil together in the house, but notices nothing untoward. As the videowala departs, Sushil goes to the telephone in the outer room of their small flat. Bringing the receiver to his ear, he presses the redial button and listens silently. A man answers with a "hello" at the other end. Sushil immediately recognizes Matloob Karim's voice. His heart chills and then hardens as he replaces the receiver.

Seething, he strides into the bedroom and confronts Naina. Why, he asks, is she still carrying on with Matloob? Why has she not shunned him and put an end to their relationship? Naina replies curtly that it is none of his business. He has absolutely no right to interfere in her private life, she says acidly.

Naina's retort adds fuel to Sushil's burning anger, which is fast growing to levels beyond his control. He feels anguished, his thoughts are straying towards the irrational – as they have so many times in the past, when he has entertained a desire to be rid of her. His mind has time and again toyed with various scenarios, juggling and weighing the different possibilities, the avenues and means by which he can eliminate her.

He observes Naina and finds her in a suitably inebriated state. The liquor that has emboldened his agitated mind has merely stupefied hers. A dark inner voice, the kind that a man in his senses recoils from, goads him to act: Now is the time to do it.

How he murdered

Quietly he goes to the chest of drawers, opens one, takes out his revolver and inspects it, then loads it with four cartridges. In cold blood, without a second thought, he turns around and aims at Naina's head, firing three times at point-blank range. Two of the bullets find their mark in Naina's

  Top Criminal Cases That Shocked The India

head and neck. The third bullet misses and hits the plywood by the air conditioner. Naina falls, bleeding profusely. She writhes in pain on the bed for a moment, and is still. She dies almost instantaneously.

The drone and rattle of desert coolers and the assortment of sounds within the flats – of ordinary family life and favourite Sunday television soap operas – continue unabated even after Naina's killing. The noise of the discharging pistol and the bullet ricocheting against the bedroom wall is lost in the din of colony life; not one neighbour hears the fatal shots. Though the inhabitants of the four-storeyed tenements live cheek by jowl, everyone remains oblivious to the end of a promising young life in their midst – at least until the police descend on the apartment block in force and newspapers break the story a day later.

Sushil's act after the murder

Sushil gathers his wits about him. He calms his nerves by drinking cold water from the fridge. His mind is racing, contemplating the next move: how to dispose of Naina's body.

The first thought that comes to his mind is to dump the body into the river Yamuna. That, he feels, should be easy. And then he can make good his escape. Escape? Where to? Well, that's secondary – first things first!

He looks around him and acts hurriedly, making a desperate attempt to remove all signs of the killing. He bundles up the body in the same bed sheet on which Naina had fallen and then wraps it in the plastic sheet that covers the dining table. He washes the room to clean it of the splattered blood, and changes his own bloodstained clothes. Peering outside, he satisfies himself that there is no one around and that nobody has been alarmed by the sound of gunfire.

He scurries downstairs and backs his Maruti close to the staircase, then runs back to the apartment. He drags the bundle with the dead body through the flat to the main door, the connecting first-floor corridor, and then down the stairs to the ground floor. Folding down the rear seat of his 800cc white Maruti car, he hoists the bundle into the dickey.

Sushil's silken white 'kurta- pyjama' is badly stained. Blood had spattered on it the moment he shot Naina. He has smeared it further while hauling her corpse through the apartment, down the stairs and into the car. He hurries upstairs to the apartment and changes into another white kurta pyjama. Back in the car in no time, he drives away. It is now past 9.30pm on Sunday, July 2, 1995.

Whether by divine dispensation or coincidence, Jagdev Singh, a neighbour from the next block, witnesses Sushil loading the bundle into the dickey. Amba Dass, a head constable patrolling in the area, sees Sushil driving away in his car. Neither man thinks much of it until later.

Sushil drives from Mandir Marg to Kali Bari and Gole Dak Khana, down Ashoka Road to Firoz Shah Road and onwards. Turning right past the Railway Tilak Bridge, he drives along Indraprastha Marg, past the front of Delhi Police Headquarters plaza and reaches the ITO bridge, which stretches across the broad, polluted expanse of the Yamuna river and its floodplains to Vikas Marg.

But his hopes of ridding himself of the body in the Yamuna are now dashed. The bridge is full of traffic and heavily congested, with vehicles moving bumper to bumper, even at this late hour. He realizes that he will almost certainly be exposed and apprehended should he attempt to dump the body into the river.

Sushil's mind is working overtime for a solution. In a sudden brainwave, he thinks of the tandoor at the Bagiya restaurant. Yes, he tells himself, he can dispose of the body by burning it on the tandoor. At the end of the bridge over the Yamuna, he performs a U-turn and drives back to Ashoka Road.

Sushil reaches the Bagiya at 10.15 pm and parks his car in the parking space just inside the main gate. Mahesh Prasad, a security guard, sees the car enter and makes the relevant entry of the car number along with the time of arrival in the register. Philip Paul, who performs at the Bagiya in the evenings with his wife Nisha, is entering the restaurant and notices Sushil in the car.

Keshav Kumar – Co –accused and the manager of the Bagiya Bareque.

Sushil beckons Keshav Kumar, the manager of the Bagiya Barbeque, and tells him that there has been a major mishap – that he has committed a massive blunder. He wants the restaurant to be closed quickly and the staff sent off, so he can dispose of the incriminating bundle by burning it on the tandoor.

Keshav understands. He is horrified, disgusted even, but his loyalty to Sushil compels him to go inside the restaurant and act on his boss's command. This man has seen him through some of the most difficult times of his life, and he will not desert him now.

Karan Singh, Sushil's former employee, sees Sushil speaking to Keshav in the car. He comes to the car to greet him, broaching the subject of some outstanding wages. Sushil fobs him off by asking him to come another day and take the payment. Karan leaves.

Sushil continues to remain seated in the car, watched by Sultan Singh, one of the security guards, who is standing near the hotel gate. In the meantime, Keshav asks the customers present in the restaurant to finish their dinner quickly. He extinguishes the restaurant lights, even as they gulp down the remainder of their food. A customer, Narendra Nath Gupta, is astonished to find himself suddenly sitting in a darkened restaurant. The patrons are effectively forced to leave.

Keshav asks all the staff and workers too, to leave for the day. Philip and Nisha, the husband-wife duo, are surprised. They see Sushil sitting in the car as they leave. The staff members are given ₹25 each by Keshav in lieu of the dinner normally provided to them at the restaurant.

Once the customers and the staff have left, Keshav approaches Sushil, who reverses the car to the steps of the restaurant. Keshav brings a large black polythene tarpaulin and together they unload the bundle from the dickey onto the tarpaulin. They carry it straight to the kitchen area and place it next to the tandoor. In the process, Keshav's clothes are stained here and there with blood. It is now around 10.50pm.

Sushil asks Keshav to draw the 'kanaat' and fixes it to block the entry to the restaurant. They then pick up a few wooden planks that are piled on the grass around the chairs in front of the restaurant, and break them into smaller pieces. They pick up other items of wood and party propaganda material and arrange these like a pyre around the body, still bundled in the bed sheet. They place it atop the tandoor. They pile more wood around and above the bundle. Keshav then leaves at Sushil's behest and returns with four large packs of Amul butter. He places them on the bundle with the body. It is now a little past 11 pm. Sushil sets the pyre alight, consigning Naina's body to the flames.

As Naina's body burns, Sushil pauses, the first time he has done so in the preceding two hours. He places his pistol on a table and pours several glasses of cold water over his head, to cool himself and wash away the mortal sin he has just committed. "Yeh maine kya kar diya? Yeh mujhse kya ho gaya?" (What have I done? How could I have done this?) The expression of regret, if it is 'regret', comes far too late. He pours more cold water over himself.

Keshav stokes the blazing fire, while Sushil positions himself near the entrance at the 'kanaat'. The revolver is still in his pocket; if need be, he will use it again. The rising flames from the makeshift pyre leap high and the billowing smoke is visible in the night sky over the Bagiya – high and far enough to catch the attention of those in the vicinity. The vegetable vendor across the lane, the elderly Anaro Devi, is alarmed by the leaping flames. As is constable Kunju, who is on patrol and catches sight of them from a distance.

Matloob Karim – Naina Sahini

The case sprang from a love triangle with a happy beginning and tragic denouement. It all started with Naina Sahni and Matloob Karim, both class-mates and N.S.U.I leaders, falling in love. They could not marry, however, owing to stiff resistance from their parents. Later, Naina came in contact with Sushil Sharma, also a college mate and Delhi Youth Congress leader. Their acquaintance grew into a love affair and later culminated in marriage. Her murder on July 2, 1995, allegedly by her husband, who burnt her body in a tandoor at Bagia restaurant, a part of Ashoka Hotel Yatri Niwas run by him, shook the whole country and left the Capital benumbed.

Trial in the Court

Out of the 43 witnesses examined, 26 have supported the prosecution theory that Naina was murdered by Sushil Sharma. Prominent among those who have corroborated the prosecution version are Matloob Karim, Mr. K.K Tuli, General Manager of Hotel Yatri Niwas, Mr. Philip, a singer in the restaurant, Mr. V.N Sehgal, Director C.F.S.L (since retired), Mr. D.K Rao, a senior IAS officer of the Gujarat cadre with whom Sharma stayed in Gujarat Bhavan after committing the crime and Dr. Bharat Singh of the M.S Civil Hospital who had conducted the postmortem.

The remaining 17 witnesses either turned hostile or were dropped on being "won over" by the defense. They include Mr. Jagdish Taneja, who had supplied cassettes to the deceased on the day of occurrence, Mr. Karam

Singh, an employee of Sushil Sharma, Mr. M.S William, an employee of Gujarat Bhavan, and Mr Sat Pal and Mr. Parminder Singh, both taxi drivers who had allegedly helped Sushil Sharma to escape from Delhi after committing the crime.

Mr. K.K. Sood, senior advocate appointed by the court to defend the accused, asserts that Sharma is innocent. He has been framed, he says. There are many loose ends in the prosecution theory. The prosecution has fabricated a plethora of useless circumstances. A large number of witnesses have been given up. Only docile witnesses who were amenable, he says, to public influence for various reasons, have corroborated the police theory.

After completing the investigation in a record time of less than a month, the Delhi police had slapped a 19-page charge-sheet on Sushil Sharma on July 27,1995. Penned in Hindi, the charge-sheet alleges that the accused suspected his wife's fidelity. He thought that she was still maintaining her relationship with Matloob Karim. This suspicion led to a discord between them. More often than not, he used to bash her up. Another reason for the discord was that while Sushil wanted to keep his marriage with Naina a secret affair, Naina used to say that they should make it public.

Sushil's immediate provocation to kill Naina on July 2, 1995, says the charge-sheet, was that when he reached his flat (No 8/2-A, D.I.Z. Area, Mandir Marg), he saw Naina consuming liquor and conversing with someone on the telephone. When he entered the house, she put down the receiver. Sushil suspected that she was talking to Matloob Karim and re-dialled the number. His suspicion was confirmed when Karim responded at the other end.

Sushil was incensed and fired three shots from his licensed revolver. While one bullet pierced through Naina's head, the other hit her in the neck. The third bullet missed her and hit the air conditioner. Naina died on the spot. Later he bundled the body of Naina into his Maruti car and stuffed it in the oven of his restaurant. That night he stayed with his I.A.S friend, D.K Rao, at Gujarat Bhavan.

The next day Sushil escaped to Jaipur. From there, he first went to Bombay and later Madras and obtained anticipatory bail. A police party led by the Additional Police Commissioner, Mr Maxwell Pereira, air-dashed to Madras. Sushil then fled to Bangalore, where he surrendered on July 10. He was arrested and brought to Delhi.

Forensic - FSL

The police seized his revolver and blood-stained clothes and sent them to the Lodhi Road Forensic Laboratory. They also took blood sample of Naina's parents, Mr. Harbhajan Singh and Mrs. Jaswant Kaur, and sent them to Hyderabad for DNA test.

The Forensic Laboratory report, reproduced in the charge-sheet, says: "Blood sample preserved by the doctor while conducting the postmortem and the blood stains on two leads recovered from the skull and neck of the body of deceased Naina are of "B" blood group."

The DNA test report, also incorporated in the charge-sheet, says: "The tests prove beyond any reasonable doubt that the charred body is that of Naina Sahni who is the biological offspring of Mr. Harbhajan Singh and Mrs. Jaswant Kaur."

The charge-sheet adds that the police had recovered a letter which Naina wrote to Sushil. The letter, inter alia, says: "I know you hate me and cannot accept me. Do not waste your time. Take care of your life. Forgive me. Leave me to my fate. Do not suspect me. I know I do not deserve you. Do not say anything to my parents. They are innocent. Inflict any punishment on me that you deem fit."

IV. LEGAL AND STATUTORY ISSUES

1.   The motive of the crime was on grounds of Sharma doubting his wife's character. The Legal issue involved here was that the case was put up on **the basis of circumstantial evidence** (DNA) and second **autopsy**. The accused was proved guilty on grounds of these only.

2.   Strained interpersonal relationship between husband and wife led to the outrage, further sudden provocation, in a fit of rage which made him commit such a heinous crime.

3.   Conspiracy to cause destruction of evidence of murder.

4.   **Section 34 of the Indian Penal Code** says, when a criminal act is done by several persons with that of a common intention of all, each of such person is liable for that act in the same manner as if it were done by him alone. Also **Section 37 of IPC** says intentional cooperation in a commission of an offence of another also constitutes an offence; which was the case with Sushil Sharma (the accused) and Keshav Kumar (restaurant employee).

5.   **Section 120 B of IPC** talks about punishment of Criminal conspiracy. The very act of Keshav Kumar who helped Sharma burn the pieces of the corpse in the Tandoor constituted his facilitation of the murder and later helped him flee from the crime scene, hence liable for punishment.

6.   Keshav Kumar (the co-accused) who helped Sushil disappear from the restaurant and also helped him destroy the corpse was also charged under the **Section 201 of IPC** because he caused the disappearance of evidence with the intention of hiding Sushil from legal action and also he lied about the burning saying it to be old Congress posters, therefore gave an information to the police which was false.

7.   Sushil Sharma had a very smooth escape from the restaurant with the aid of Keshav Kumar which comes under **Section 212** which says harboring an offender with the intention to screen him from legal punishment shall be punished as mentioned in the Section.

8.   Punishment for murder under **Section 302 of IPC** which says whoever commits the murder is to be punished with death or imprisonment for life and will also be liable to fine.

ANALYSIS AND COMPARISION

Points to be pondered on

1.   This was a clear case of homicidal death of a wife who was murdered by the husband in a fit of rage because of him doubting her having an affair. However the case took over a decade to bring out the proper judgment. The question which thus strikes in the minds of people is "Why would such a case take that long to decide?" The answer is quite clear. Political influence always plays a vital role in this system. When the accused is the President of Delhi Youth Congress, it is pretty much evident that one might use his influence for turning the tables.

2.   However, Sushil Sharma never denied the fact that he killed his wife; what he does deny that he chopped his wife to pieces and then burnt her in Tandoor. In an interview he said "That one day is blur in my life. Till today, I do not know what happened. It happened in a fraction of a second and that one second has cost me 20 years."

3.   The repeated mention of a strained relationship between the accused and deceased came about to be an important parameter for the final judgment. The reason for tensions between the couple was that Sushil was reluctant to disclose their marriage and accept her as his wife publically, and the reason so given was that it would have affected his political career which is very difficult to digest. In any case, marriage can hardly spoil anyone's political prospects. However, this was a strong motive behind the murder.

JUDGEMENT AND SUGGESTIONS

In 2003, Sharma was awarded with death penalty by a district court. He appealed in **the Delhi High Court** for the same where he found no mercy and the judgment of the Court said in 2007:

"People like the appellant who are power drunk and have no value for human life are definitely a menace for the society at large and deserve no mercy. ... The act of the appellant is so abhorrent and dastardly that in case death penalty is not awarded to him it would be a mockery of justice and conscience of the society at large would be shocked. This is surely a case which falls within the category of 'rarest of rare cases' in which no other punishment except the death penalty would be justified."

What comes next it the Supreme Court's judgment in 2014 stating:

"Undoubtedly the offence is brutal but the brutality alone would not justify the death sentence in this case."

Is this judgment not a mockery of justice? Does this not shock the conscience of the society at large?

Death sentence awarded by the trial court, confirmed by the High Court and finally commuted by the Supreme Court to life imprisonment

INTRODUCTION

Almost every person   breaks some rule even if just once . This can be defined as criminal behavior but not everyone who has broken the rule can be defined as a criminal. Specifically in India, 2007 has turned out to be a year that has brought   kidnapping, rape, necrophilia and cannibalism in the limelight. . Surender Koli had been accused of that cannibalistic criminality. He is just like other normal people; even he has one wife and two children who live hundreds of kilometers away in a Himalayan village.

It came into the public spotlight after its appearance in an Indian serial **"House of Horrors"** that could lay claim to being a house where 16 victims had met their end. They are also known as the Noida serial murders or Nithari massacre because they occurred in Noida, or more accurately in Nithari that is a region of Noida.. As we know Noida is a systematically planned Indian city under the management of 'New Okhla Industrial Development Authority' this comes inUttar Pradesh, India. The **Noida serial murders** (also **Nithari serial murders** or **Nithari Kand**) occurred in the house of businessman Moninder Singh Pandher in Sector-31, Noida, near Nithari village, Uttar Pradesh, India between 2005 and 2006. Moninder Singh was convicted in two out of the five cases against him and his servant Surinder Koli who aided him was convicted in 10 out of the 16 cases against him. Both were sentenced to death.

Chronology House of Horror in India

In December 2006, two Nithari village residents reported they knew the location of the remains of children who had gone missing in the previous two years: the municipal water tank behind house D5, Sector-31, Noida. Both had daughters who were missing, and they suspected Surinder Koli, the domestic help at D5, was involved in the disappearances. The residents claimed they had been repeatedly ignored by local authorities; therefore, they sought the help of former Resident Welfare Association (RWA) President S. C. Mishra. That morning, Mishra and the two residents searched the tank drain. One of the residents claimed to have found a decomposed hand, after which they contacted the police.

It is a strange case because no one ever , including the owner of the house, knew that his domestic assistance, Surender Koli, was committing crimes in his house. The background goes back to 2003, when an abnormally high number of women and children were reported missing from Nithari village in Noida district. The phenomenon of missing children was in line with arrival Surender Koli in Moninder Pandher's home at D-5, Noida. Some parents who lost their children had reported to the police but the local police paid no attention to their complaints.. Then in 2005, 14 years old Rimpa Haldar went missing on 8 February. Her parents tried to register the case with the police but their effort was unsuccessful. Next month some boys was playing cricket, found a hand in a plastic bag in an open area behind house no.D-5 .They called the police, who after seeing the hand, advised them to forget about it, and no action was taken. The next year, a 20 years old girl named Payal went missing on May 7, that heightened the assumption of Koli being connected with the missing of this girl and other people.

Finally the disappearance of the children was reported in the High Court and the police were directed to investigate the matter. They searched Moninder Pandher's home based on the reports of local residents who were distrustful with Koli's presence in that house . In this phase, Surender Koli was suspected as being the person behind the missing of so many people in the last few years. Police claimed that it was through Koli that they discovered the large number of skulls and bones in the open space at the back of D-5, and in the drain running on the main road in front of the bungalows. Thus, Koli was arrested on 29 December 2006.

HOW KOLI KILLED THE VICTIMS

To tell truth the victims of Koli increased with the passage time. In his latest confession, Koli revealed that he lured the children into the house by offering them sweets and chocolates.

So how was Koli carrying out his criminal activities since it was not just his home, but his domestic full time servant and his wife also lived there. e Pandher's wife often travelled to Chandigarh, and Pandher would be at work almost during the day. After each killing, Koli would strip the clothes of his victim and carry the body upstairs to a bathroom where he would proceed to chop it into small parts.

Koli gave the details of how exactly he lured a total of 16 victims (9 female children, 2 male children and 5 adult women) into the house, killed and attempted to have sex with the inert bodies, chopped and ate their body parts, and then threw the remains at the back of the house and in the drain on the main road. It was also reported Koli's way to lure children into the house was by offering them sweets and chocolates.

Then he would leave the bathroom in that condition while he cooked and ate some of the body parts. After 3-4 hours when he would regain his composure, only then would he would clean up the drawing room and bathroom. In the investigation, CBI did not find clear motives regarding this cannablistic criminality. In one of the investigations, he admitted to eating human organs in the belief that cannibalism cured impotency, but on the other hand his wife said that Koli did not have suffer from impotency. Koli admitted to killing a call girl for refusing to have sex with him, and had sex with the corpse to prevent feeling rejected. His desire to having sex can also be a cause because Pandher often called girls into his house. Hence some observers view Koli as a really shrewd and cunning person, because he could cover his crime perfectly.

Events leading to primary investigation

In December 2006, two Nithari village residents reported they knew the location of the remains of children who had gone missing in the previous two years: the municipal water tank behind house D5, Sector-31, Noida. Both had daughters who were missing, and they suspected Surinder Koli, the domestic help at D5, was involved in the disappearances. The residents claimed they had been repeatedly ignored by local authorities; therefore, they sought the help of former Resident Welfare Association (RWA) President S C Mishra. That morning, Mishra and the two residents searched the tank drain. One of the residents claimed to have found a decomposed hand, after which they contacted the police.

Anxious parents of children missing in the last two years rushed to Nithari with photographs. Koli, under the alias Satish, later confessed to killing six children and a 20-year-old woman referred to as "Payal" after sexually assaulting them.

DISCOVERY AND INSEPCTION

The families of the missing children accused the police of negligence. Initially, some police officers, including Noida SP city, denied any criminal angle and asserted that the families had provided false information about the ages of the missing; that they weren't minors but instead were adults who left home after fighting with their parents. The residents also alleged that the police were corrupt and were paid to conceal information. Demands were made for an independent investigation. One of the residents asserted that the police were claiming credit for discovering the bodies when it was the residents who dug them up. The police denied having found fifteen bodies, reiterating that they had discovered skulls, bones and other body parts, and said they were unable to give a figure for the number of victims. The victims' identities and number could only be established with DNA tests. The police then sealed the house and did not allow news media near the site.

The Central government tried to ascertain the facts behind the discovery of the skeletal remains and whether it had "inter-state ramifications". Law and order are State matters, but the Home Ministry asked for details about the magnitude of the crime.

Q On 26 and 27 December respectively, Koli's employer, Moninder Singh Pandher, and Koli were taken into custody by the police in connection with the disappearance of "Payal". After Koli's confession, the police started digging up the nearby land area and discovered the children's bodies.

Two policemen were suspended on 31 December for failing to take action despite being informed about a number of children missing, as angry residents charged the house of the alleged mastermind, demanding the removal of the Mulayam Singh government.

The situation at Nithari was aggravated as an angry mob of villagers fought with police, the pelting stones at each other, just outside the residence of the accused. The police also detained Pandher's maid Maya under suspicion that she lured women to the house. As more body parts were dug up near the premises, hundreds of local residents descended on the spot and alleged that there was an organ trade connection to the grisly killings of young children. A doctor living close to the Pandher residence, Navin Choudhary, had been under police suspicion a few years prior in connection with an alleged kidney racket at his hospital. Searches were conducted throughout his properties, and the investigators found no evidence to support the claim.

Primary investigation

On 1 January 2007, the remand magistrate granted the police custody of Pandher and Koli until 10 January 2007, as the investigators said that further interrogation was required to complete the recovery of victims' remains. The court also granted permission for Narco Analysis. On the same evening, police conducted a raid on Pandher's Chandigarh residence. His wife and son were interrogated about Pandher's habits. Police sources disclosed that their relationship with him was "strained", which was later found untrue. His behaviour was described as normal. A senior police inspector revealed that there would be a series of searches conducted at Pandher's Ludhiana farmhouse and nearby places. The recent child kidnapping cases in Chandigarh - Pandher's hometown - were re-opened, but nothing was found.

The next day, 15 of the 17 skeletons discovered in the village were identified. Ten of them were identified by Koli when he was confronted with the photographs of the missing children. Five others were identified by family members after being shown belongings recovered from the scene. The torsos of the bodies were missing and the investigating team was looking into possibilities that the killings were motivated by illicit trade in human organs. The police said that there were at least 31 child victims.

Security was increased as police expected more disturbance, following two days of violence near Pandher's residence. In a press statement, Chief Justice of India Y. K. Sabharwal asserted that the investigation was at a preliminary level, and neither the courts nor the Central Bureau of Investigation (CBI) were involved at that point.

Forensic – DNA

The panel met the parents of the victims to record their statements even as the police determined that out of the 17 confirmed people killed, 10 were girls. Parents of eight of the sexually abused children were given compensation of Rs. 12 lakhs. The DNA samples from the human remains were sent to a forensic laboratory in Hyderabad for the identification of the victims while forensic samples were sent to the laboratory in Agra for determining the age, cause of death and other details. It was determined that "Payal" was the only adult victim identified, with all other 11 victims below the age of 10. Seven of the eight families that had been provided compensation of Rs. 200,000 on 3 January 2007, returned their cheques in protest. However, the cheques were soon returned to them. They demanded houses and jobs in compensation as well.

LODGING OF FIR

An FIR had been filed on 7 October 2006. Investigations revealed that Payal's cellphone was being used although the SIM card she owned remained inactive. Through digital surveillance, the investigators were able to track down a number of people and could finally reach the man who sold the phone. The rickshaw cart puller affirmed that the phone belonged to someone from the Pandher residence. After the affirmation of the facts by the witness, Moninder Singh was called for interrogation, which subsequently revealed nothing. His aide and servant, Surinder Koli was picked up the next day and he confessed killing the woman and dumping her body behind the house. The police started digging and henceforth recovered the skeletal remains of the missing children instead of Payal.

Nand Lal, the father of the girl – Deepika alias Payal, alleged that the police had threatened and harassed him. He stated that it was because of the court intervention that the police officers registered the FIR.

Suspicions of child pornography

The investigating teams seized erotic literature along with a laptop computer connected to a webcam, which immediately raised apprehensions of the presence of an international child pornography racket. The police also recovered photographs of Pandher with nude children and foreigners during his four international visits. It was alleged that Pandher supplied such pictures abroad and could link him to pedophilia, which was later discovered to be untrue. Later during the investigation it was found that the nude children in the pictures were Pandher's grandchildren. There was no link found to child pornography] The laptop and the webcam were later returned to the family, and the story was classified as a media-created rumour.

CONFESSION OF EATING VICTIMS BODY

The police initially suspected an organ trade angle as to the motive behind the murders and raided the house of a doctor who lived in the neighbourhood of the primary accused. A team of officials, accompanied by a team of forensic experts, went to pick up possible evidence for tests. The police revealed that the doctor had been accused of a similar crime in 1998, although the court had absolved him the same year. There was a second raid a few days later. The police were, however, cautious with the news reports suggesting the accused committed cannibalism even before the polygraph tests had barely begun. They were "aghast" when they learned of media reports that one of the accused had confessed to the consumption of the victims' livers and other body parts.

CASE TRANSFERRED TO CBI

In January 2007 the case was transferred to the Central Bureau of Investigation (CBI) that took Koli's custody thereafter. The Investigation had been transferred because local police failed in their duty to respond to complaints over the past two years. First investigations by CBI team visits Nithari to initiate probe in the case. 30 more bones found near the house. The court process taken until three years to give Surender Koli death sentence as the case was classified as 'rarest of rare'. I find the data records related in missing children and also person around Noida district with the person admitted as killed by accused:

To tell the truth the victims of Koli kept increasing with passage time. In his latest confession, it was also reported that Koli used to to lure the children into the house by offering them sweets and chocolates.

The reports were incriminating and proclaimed that the local police failed in their duty to respond to complaints over the past two years. The discovery of several polythene bags containing parts of human torsos led the investigators to conclude that it was unlikely that the accused had links to illegal organ trade. The CBI team discovered the bags in the drains outside the Pandher residence. After interrogating Surinder Koli, they came to a prima facie conclusion that "he is a psychopath used to carry out the killings". Interrogators also said that it was possible that Pandher had no role to play in the murders. The seized materials were sent to laboratory for post-mortem, identification , and DNA extraction. The materials received from the Uttar Pradesh police were also forwarded for forensic examination. Some liquor bottles, a double-barreled gun, cartridges, mobile phones, photographs, photo albums and a blood-stained grill were handed over to the CBI for extensive examination. Preliminary investigations revealed that the bones were not more than two years old. The CBI also revealed that only fifteen skulls had been found thus far, and not seventeen as claimed by the state police.

A three-member CBI team questioned the kin of Surinder Koli in the Almora district. In November 2007, the Supreme Court notified the CBI concerning the case about the allegation by a relative of a victim that the investigating agency was trying to shield Moninder Singh Pandher, one of the key accused in the case.

VICTIMS

Payal was the only adult victim in the string of serial murders. Young girls constituted the majority of victims. Post-mortem reports of the 17 sets of skulls and bones recovered showed that 11 of the killed were girls. Doctors at Noida Government Hospital revealed that there was a "butcher-like precision" in the chopping of the bodies. The post mortem reports revealed that there had been a pattern in the killings. A gory revelation was made by the AIIMS on 6 February 2007. It was also concluded that there were 19 skulls in all; 16 complete and 3 damaged. The bodies had been cut into three pieces before being disposed of by the servant. The CBI sources said that the manservant, after strangling the victims, severed their heads and threw them in the drain behind the house of his employer. Sources also revealed that he used to keep the viscera in a polythene bag before disposing of it in a drain, so as to prevent detection. The skulls and the other remains were forwarded to the Centre for DNA Fingerprinting and Diagnostics, Hyderabad for further profiling. The crime scene examination, recovery and collection of human remains and exhibits and their detailed examination was carried out by experts from AIIMS and CFSL under the chairmanship and guidance of professor

Convictions

On 12 February 2009, both the accused—Moninder Singh Pandher and his domestic servant Surinder Koli—were found guilty of the 8 February 2005 murder of Rimpa Haldar, 14, by a special sessions court in Ghaziabad. This verdict left the Central Bureau of Investigation (CBI) red faced, as the CBI had earlier given a clean chit to Moninder Singh Pandher in all its charge sheets. Both the accused Moninder Singh Pandher and Surinder Koli were given the death sentence on 13 February 2009, as the case was classified as "rarest of rare".

•   On 4 May 2010, Koli was found guilty of the 25 October 2006 murder of Arti Prasad, 7, and given a second death sentence eight days later.

- On 27 September 2010, Koli was found guilty of the 10 April 2006 murder of Rachna Lal, 9, and given a third death sentence the following day.

- On 22 December 2010, Koli was found guilty of the June 2006 murder of Deepali Sarkar, 12, and given a fourth death sentence.

- On 15 February 2011, the Supreme Court upheld the death sentence of Surinder Koli

- On 24 December 2012, Koli was found guilty of the 4 June 2005 murder of Chhoti Kavita, 5, and given a fifth death sentence. In February 2011, The Supreme Court of India upheld their death sentence. In July 2014,

PRESIDENT OF INDIA REJECTED MERCY PETITIONS

- The President of India rejected the mercy petitions filed by Koli On 3 September 2014, the Court issued a death warrant against Koli in Nithari case. On the evening of 4 September 2014 Surinder Koli was transferred to Meerut Jail because of the absence of hanging facilities at Dasna Jail, Ghaziabad. He was to be hanged on 12 September 2014.

Acquittal

On 10 September 2009, the Allahabad high court acquitted Moninder Singh Pandher and overturned his death sentence. He was not named a main suspect by investigators initially, but was summoned as co-accused during the trial. Pandher faces trial in five cases out of the remaining 12, and could be re-sentenced to death if found guilty in any of those killings. The same day Pandher was acquitted, the Allahabad high court upheld the death sentence for Surinder Koli, the former domestic servant of Pandher. On 24 July 2017, both Koli and Pandher have been given the death.

The Mathura Rape Case Of 1972

INTRODUCTION

But rape knows no boundaries of class or culture.

After it happened, she might as well have worn a scarlet label on her chest. Such was the stigma of rape in India then. She was brave to speak out and did what few women back then did. She took her case to court.

Mathura, a young tribal woman from Maharashtra, was reportedly raped by two uniformed police officers in 1972. Her trauma shook the country and changed the landscape of **rape laws** in India.

The **Mathura rape case** was an incident of custodial rape in India on 26 March 1972, wherein Mathura, a young tribal girl, was allegedly raped by two policemen in the compound of Desaiganj Police Station in Gadchiroli district of Maharashtra. After the Supreme Court acquitted the accused, there was public outcry and protests, which eventually led to amendments in the Indian rape law via The Criminal Law Amendment Act 1983.

Madhura – Victim

Mathura, a young tribal woman from Maharashtra was an orphan living with one of her two brothers, she was between 14 and 16 years old at that time. Mathura occasionally worked as a domestic helper with a woman named Noshi. Desaiganj was the town where she lived when she was raped. Nobody gave importance to what was happening within the society. Nor would they stand up against injustice done to others. That's why cases of rape were buried by people in those days. Whether it was rape or murder, most cases went unreported."

But Mathura wanted the perpetrators punished. She pressed charges, knowing how difficult it would be for her in court. It would be her word against that of two policemen.

"She was pretty. Fair-skinned, She was simple-natured." Her parents died when she was young and she, not surprisingly, learned to fend for herself.

She lived with one of her two brothers, Gama, who herded cattle and did various other menial jobs. Mathura made money as a maid.

Childhood Friends and her relation with Ashok (her lover)

Motiram Meshram

Mathura's relatives and friends, including a man named Motiram Meshram, lived in Desaiganj. He had known Mathura since her childhood. Motiram He testified against the two policemen she said had raped her. Meshram was a socially conservative man who probably did not make much of Mathura's rape, maybe even blamed her in some way or justified it like the police inspector did.

At 65, Meshram ha done better than many. He has raised two sons and a daughter and ma a living farming rice. He own a tractor and a two-room house that even ha an air cooler inside, although it of no use on sultry days when the air thick with dampness. Still, it a relief to be out of the sun's punishing glare. (Changes were made but they are not required)

But many of the huts in the Shivaji Ward ha been replaced by brick and mortar homes like Meshram's. Back at Meshram's house, the three goats tied up to posts and the roaming roosters bristle at the afternoon interruption.

Four decades ago, says Shantibai, men were good for nothing. They sat at home with their hooch, got drunk and then abused their girlfriends and wives, the sole wage earners in the family. She suspects Mathura may have suffered the same habit.

ASHOK (HER LOVER)

Ashok is no longer alive. But Meshram has asked Ashok's cousin, Ganesh Kodape, to come over and speak with me. Ganesh is 54 now, has skin the color of coffee beans and large eyes that are fierce and gentle all at once. He dropped out of school after the second grade. He says everyone in his family -- including Ashok -- was poor, so poor that Ganesh didn't wear any clothes as a boy.

He was only 13 or 14 when Mathura was attacked, and he doesn't remember it well. But he tells me Ashok worked as a manual laborer.

Mathura and Ashok fell in love. They developed an intimate relationship and decided they would one day marry. Ganesh remembers

Nushi treated Mathura as a daughter-in-law. In tribal communities, Mathura's relationship with Ashok was not unheard of. But in the larger Indian society, she was a tainted woman for being single and sexually active. When she was between 14-16 years old, she had developed a relationship with Ashok, a man who was related to her employer. As per the customary practice of her tribe, Mathura had eloped with Ashok and was living with him.

Mathura's brother did not approve.

Gama, according to court documents, lodged a complaint with the police that his sister had been abducted by Ashok and his family; that she was forced into prostitution. Either he didn't believe Mathura was in love or he was embarrassed by the relationship and wanted to break it up.

Meshram remembers the night when police summoned Mathura to the station. She was required to make a statement regarding her brother's complaint. Then Meshram tells me something I didn't know from reading accounts of the case. He tells me that he accompanied Mathura to the police station.

"You were there the night she was raped?" "Yes," he says.

Background

The **incident** took place on 26 March 1972, in Desaiganj Maharashtra. Mathura, who at the time was between 14-16 years old, had developed a relationship with Ashok, a man who was related to her employer. As per customary practice of her tribe, Mathura had eloped with Ashok and was living with him. Mathura was an orphan and lived with her brother Gama prior to this.

"Among several tribes in the Western India- Rajasthan, Gujarat and Maharashtra, the live-in relationships between couples is a customary practice. Their culture of cohabitation is based on couple's right to choose and right to reject. Bhils in Gujarat, Garasia, Gamar Community in Rajasthan who are subsisting on farming and manual labour have been extremely poor and deprived for centuries. They have traditionally been cohabiting under live-in arrangements, have children also and when they accumulate adequate marriage expenses, they get married. At times the head of the household organizes group-marriages of 2 generations of live-in couples to economize the cost," said Dr. Vibhuti Patel, women's study scholar.

  Top Criminal Cases That Shocked The India

On the day of incident

She met Noshi's nephew named Ashok who wanted to marry her, but her brother did not agree to the union and went to the local police station to lodge a complaint claiming that his sister, a minor, was being kidnapped by Ashok and his family members. After receiving the complaint, the police authority brought Ashok and his family members to the police station. Following general investigation, Mathura, her brother, Ashok, and his family members were permitted to go back home. However, as they were leaving,

When her relatives and the assembled crowd threatened to burn down the police chowky, the two accused policemen, Ganpat and Tukaram, reluctantly agreed to file a panchnama (legal recording of evidence).

Constable Ganpat took Mathura to a toilet situated near the back of the building, loosened her underwear and shone a torch over her private parts. He then dragged her to the main building where he pushed her to the ground and raped her in spite of stiff resistance on her part. After Ganpat, constable Tukaram also came over Mathura and fondled her private parts. He too tried to rape her, but was unable to do so because he was highly intoxicated at the time.

By this time Mathura's family, who had been waiting outside the police station started to grow suspicious since the lights of the police station had been turned off and the entrance was bolted from within. They called out to Mathura but received no response, and the noise attracted a crowd near the station. After some time Mathura emerged from the station and informed the crowd that she had been compelled by constable Ganpat to undress herself and he had then proceeded to rape her. On hearing this the agitated crowd threatened to burn down the police station, and the head constable was forced to take down Mathura's statement.

Marked twice

Mathura withdrew. She cried a lot, Meshram remembers. She couldn't concentrate.

First, poverty made her vulnerable "Then this incident broke her from within. Completely. She lost everyone who was in her life. "Mathura was marked twice: She'd had premarital sex, and she had been raped.

"Nobody gave importance to what was happening within the society. Nor would they stand up against injustice done to others. That's why cases of rape were buried by people in those days. Rape, murder. ... They went unreported."

But Mathura wanted the perpetrators punished. She pressed charges, knowing how difficult it would be for her in court. It would be her word against that of two policemen.

The defense lawyer asked why she didn't scream. Did Ganpat or Tukaram cover her mouth with their hands? Did they gag her?

"No," she replied.

In June 1974, the district court judge acquitted her assailants. He called her a "shocking liar" whose testimony was "riddled with falsehood and improbabilities." She was used to having sex and must have consented to the police, the judge said. She claimed rape so that she would appear virtuous to her lover.

The case- session court

Despite the power differential she decided to take this matter to court, and was able to do so as a young feminist lawyer, Vasudha Dhagamwar fought the case pro bono from 1972 to 1979. The case was first taken to a sessions court, which found the defendants not guilty.

The trial was held a few months later at the district court in Chandrapur. She and others who testified,

The defense lawyer asked why she didn't scream. Did Ganpat or Tukaram cover her mouth with their hands? Did they gag her?

"No," she replied.

In June 1974, the district court judge acquitted her assailants. He called her a "shocking liar" whose testimony was "riddled with falsehood and improbabilities." She was used to having sex and must have consented to the police, the judge said. She claimed rape so that she would appear virtuous to her lover.

Appeal to the Bombay High Court

The case went to the Bombay High Court in Nagpur, a city about three hours' drive from Desaiganj. On October 12, 1976, that court reversed the acquittals of the two police constables. Ganpat was sentenced to five years for rape; Tukaram got a year for the "assault or criminal force to a woman with intent to outrage her modesty."

The High Court judgement held that

"Mere passive or helpless surrender of the body and its resignation to the other's lust induced by threats or fear cannot be equated with the desire or will, nor can furnish an answer by the mere fact that the sexual act was not in opposition to such desire or volition."

Appeal to the Supreme Court

Whatever sense of justice Mathura felt was short-lived. In a 1978 appeal, the Indian Supreme Court overturned the convictions. It said Mathura must have consented because she didn't scream, and there were no visible bruises on her body.

India's rape laws at that time favored the accused. The courts did not presume a lack of consent in cases of custodial rape -- when the victim is in the custody of authorities -- as they do today. Instead the burden of proof fell on the victim, who had to convince the court she had not consented.

"No marks of injury were found on the person of the girl after the incident and their absence goes a long way to indicate that the alleged intercourse was a peaceful affair, and that the story of a stiff resistance having been put up by the girl is all false

In September 1979, the Supreme Court overturned this judgement and pronounced the defendants not guilty.

The SC's verdict was based on the following three arguments:

- Mathura did not vocally express her non-consent during the ordeal.

- There was a lack of bruising on her body.

- She was 'habituated to sexual intercourse' based on the **'two-finger-test'.**

While the first two portions of the judgement become problematic in themselves it is the third part of the judgement that raises most cause for alarm. To begin with, the two finger test—which for the longest time was the method of checking whether or not a survivor was in fact raped—is a deeply flawed process. The test is conducted by inserting two fingers inside the vagina to check the elasticity of a survivor's vagina and whether the hymen has been ruptured. Going by the number of fingers admitted, a doctor gives his opinion on whether a woman is "habituated to sex" or not. Secondly, to assume that a hymen can only be ruptured by sexual intercourse is medically incorrect. The test is not only unscientific but also illegal in India.

But more important than the medical inaccuracy of such a test is the taboo surrounding pre-marital sex. The test did not take into account cases of consensual intercourse, and by extension of that, neither did the courts. As is clearly demonstrated by this judgement, the presumption was that a woman is to only have sex after marriage, and any woman who chooses to have sex before she enters this state sanctioned institution, cannot possibly be at the receiving end of a crime such as rape.

The courts went so far as to say that since Mathura was 'habituated' to sexual intercourse, she perhaps initiated sexual intercourse, seduced the police officers, and then came out and cried rape in an effort to seem "virtuous' in front of her brother, and partner.

Civil Society response

A few days after the verdict was announced, four law professors, Upendra Baxi, Raghunath Kelkar, Lotika Sarkar and Vasudha Dhagamwar wrote an **open letter** to the Supreme Court protesting the concept of consent in the verdict. Important lines from the letter read "Is the taboo against pre-marital sex so strong as to provide a license to Indian police to rape young girls?"

Several protests and demonstrations took place in the country following this verdict, and this case is touted to be one of the cornerstones in the development of a national feminist movement in India. A number of women's group were formed as a direct response to the judgment, including 'Saheli' in Delhi, and prior to that in January 1980, in the formation of the first feminist group in India against rape, 'Forum Against Rape', later renamed 'Forum Against Oppression of Women.'

When taking a look at Mathura's case it becomes important to talk about the power structures at play. Mathura was an orphaned Adivasi teenager who was struggling to make ends meet. In her **first recounting of the incident**, Mathura said that the cops had threatened to file a false case and imprison her and her relatives if she did not do exactly as they said.

Lines from the open letter written to the Chief Justice of India, best explain the dynamics at play in the case:

 Top Criminal Cases That Shocked The India

"Your Lordship, does the Indian Supreme Court expect a young girl 14-16 years old, when trapped by two policemen inside the police station, to successfully raise an alarm for help? Does it seriously expect the girl, a labourer, to put up such stiff resistance against well-built policemen so as to have substantial marks of physical injury? Does the absence of such marks necessarily imply absence of stiff resistance?"

Legal Reform

Despite the large-scale opposition to the verdict in Mathura's case, and demanding that it be reopened, the court still held that there was no legal standing in the case to rule in favour of Mathura. Eventually this led to Government of India to **amend** the rape laws in our country. In 1983, a new category was added to criminal laws dealing with rape.

- The law mandates that a court presume a woman who says she did not consent to sexual intercourse is telling the truth.

- Mathura's case also led to in camera rape trials being conducted as closed proceedings and to a ban on identifying victims by their real names.

- Besides defining **custodial rape**, the amendment shifted the burden of proof from the accuser to the accused.

- It also demanded that before , women can not be called to the police station before sunrise and after sunset.

The never-seen-before protests that rocked India at the time of the Mathura rape case were about the tone and tenor in which the Supreme court spoke about the issue of consent – the manner in which morality and victim blaming was woven into the judgement.

Legacy

The case is seen as turning point in women right's movement in India, as it led to just greater awareness of women's legal rights issue, oppression, and patriarchal mindsets. A number of women's organizations soon came forth across India. Previously, rape misjudgments or acquittals would go unnoticed, but in the following years, women's movement against rape gathered force and organization supporting rape victims and women's rights advocates came to the fore. The criminal law amendment Act 1983 was enacted as a consequence of this case. Section 228A of the Indian Penal Code for example was enacted because of this incident.

'Millions of Mathuras'

In Delhi, Upendra Baxi read the Supreme Court's 1978 decision with utter shock. The dean of the University of Delhi law school felt compelled to speak his mind on what he believed was a travesty of justice and, more importantly, a disgrace to human rights in India. But what could he do?

He endured 10 sleepless nights before an idea sprouted: He would write an open letter to the chief justice. Rape was not a matter of national conscience in 1978. Baxi intended to make it one, for the sake of the "millions of Mathuras" who didn't even get as far as filing the first police report.

He intended to change Indian rape laws so that the burden of proof would shift away from the victim. He intended to escalate punishment for rape, to make sure the real name of a rape victim never appeared in public, to get rid of absurd metrics such as the two-finger test performed on Mathura.

His letter to the chief justice would outline all the reasons why the decision was wrong:

"What matters is a search for liberation from the colonial and male-dominated notions of what may constitute the element of consent, and the burden of proof for rape, which s many 'Mathuras' in the Indian countryside.

"Nothing short of the protection of human rights and constitutionalism is at stake."

The letter was co-signed on September 16, 1979, by three other prominent Indian lawyers.

In those days, the Supreme Court was inaccessible to most Indians. Ordinary citizens did not have the right to petition the court. Nor was it customary to pen public letters to one of the most powerful institutions in the land. No media outlet thought it newsworthy or appropriate to publish the letter.

It was only after The Dawn newspaper in Pakistan printed the letter a few months later that it appeared in the Indian media, Baxi told me. The Supreme Court did not respond, but the letter had the same kind of effect that news of the Delhi gang rape did last year, though on a smaller scale. Indians, mainly women, were shocked by the plight of Mathura.

On March 8, 1980, on International Women's Day, thousands of women marched on the streets of Delhi, Mumbai, Hyderabad and Nagpur. They included Seema Sakhare, who went on to form one of the first organizations in India to take on the issue of violence against women.

Now 80, Sakhare told me she was so taken with Mathura's case that she visited Desaiganj to see if she could help her. She even stood on a stage with Mathura at an early anti-rape rally. Then, like everyone else in India, Sakhare, too, lost touch with the woman who'd become a rallying cry for the country.

This is the legal and social history I know as I speak with the people of Desaiganj, many of them unaware of the importance of events that took place here in 1972. But Meshram knows. He knows that Mathura's name became synonymous with the changes that Baxi proposed, and the reforms that followed.

In 1983, a new category was added to criminal laws dealing with rape. When a victim is in the custody of the state, as was Mathura, the law mandates that a court presume a woman who says she did not consent is telling the truth. Mathura's case also led to rape trials being conducted as closed proceedings and to a ban on identifying victims by their real names.

Had Mathura's name not been everywhere, would she have stayed in Desaiganj? Perhaps. But as it were, she left. And only a few people from her previous life stayed in touch. One was Meshram. Over the years, he has seen Mathura only a few times .

But he never spoke publicly again of what happened -- until last December, when news of the Delhi gang rape reached Desaiganj.

"It happened here, too," he told people in the Shivaji Ward neighborhood. "Forty years ago, it happened."

No one listened. Some even thought he was getting senile, making things up.

"When is the last time you saw Mathura?"

It must have been four years ago. She saw me on the street. She was selling bamboo baskets. She recognized me and asked me to come over for a cup of tea. She seemed happy."

Four years. I wonder what has become of her since? For the first time, I dare to hope that I will find her.

I ask Meshram to take me to Nawargaon. Maybe Mathura will be open to speaking with me if she sees a familiar face.

The Burari deaths were a ritual mass suicideof eleven family members of the Chundawat family from Burari, Delhi, India, in 2018. Ten people were found hanging, while the oldest family member, the grandmother, had been strangled. The bodies were found on 1 July 2018 early in morning . The police have ruled the deaths were motivated by shared delusion or psychosis.

The Burari deaths case was a terrifying incident back in 2018 where 11-members of a family in Burari, Delhi had killed themselves. Many call it to be a case of mass suicide. While very little is known about the case, the majority of the information stands baseless or unreasonable, as has been often portrayed by television media. A family with a deep inside story was revealed to the world in a much better way, the Chundawats (familiarly called the Bhatia family), were like any other middle-class family, settled and focused on a better future. While many who viewed the family from the outside, thought they had found consolation in spirituality, there is no one left to describe what happened behind the four walls of the Burari house. The present article highlights the much-discussed case from different angles and information that were available, so as to make the reader understand the story behind the closed doors of the 11-member family.

Background

The Chundawat family (also known as Bhatia family by neighbours) had been living in the two-storey house in Burari's Sant Nagar neighbourhood for around twenty years, after moving from their native town in Tohana, Haryana.

The Chundawats were like any other middle class family, settled and focused on a better future, till a death in 2007 shook them up. While those who saw the family from outside felt they had found solace in spirituality, what happened inside the four walls of the Burari house may never be known as there is no one left to explain. "The Hindu" offers an insight into the personalities of the 11 members who died, by speaking to their relatives, friends and neighbours.

Chundawat Family's History

Move to Delhi

The Chundawat family, originally from Rajasthan, stayed in Haryana's Tohana for over a decade before moving to Delhi in 1989-90. Bhopal Singh, the husband of Narayan Devi, was a financially secure man with farmlands and cattle to rear. He sold the land and bought a plot in Burari, where he moved in with his wife and youngest son Lalit.

Bhopal Singh's only surviving son Dinesh Singh Chundawat, a building contractor in Chittorgarh, said he and Bhavnesh did not shift to Delhi at that time because of their roots in Rajasthan.

"Our entire family [relatives] was in Rajasthan, in and around Sawa village. We did not want to cut ties. Also, I liked open spaces, something which Delhi did not have. Bhavnesh and his wife came along and we thought we would set up a business together," he said. Mr. Dinesh spent eight years in Saudi Arabia from 1978-86 as a manager in a sales firm.

Visibly irritated over being called a member of the "Bhatia family" in news reports, Mr. Dinesh stressed his surname is Chundawat. "We are all Chundawats. My mother was a Bhatia from Punjab and when they [his parents] stayed there for a few years after their marriage, my father came to be known as Bhatia saab , a title which stayed with him for years," he said, adding that his sister Pratibha was married to Harinder Bhatia alias Hira, and therefore her and Priyanka's surname remained Bhatia.

Bhopal Singh, fondly called 'Daddy' by everyone close to him, was a man who commanded respect from everyone.

Helpful neighbours

"He would not even shout. His eyes were enough to let us know what we should not do," Mr. Dinesh recalled.

"He used to drink and eat non-vegetarian food. In fact, he used to cook delicious mutton dishes. But we never drank together. Whenever I visited Delhi, he used to leave a bottle of whiskey in my room for me and Bhavnesh to drink."

Why not Lalit? "Oh, he was always a teetotaller," said Mr. Dinesh.

Bhopal Singh and Narayan Devi had earned the affection of their neighbours too. "Mummy [Narayan Devi] and Daddy [Bhopal Singh] considered me their daughter. I used to tie rakhi to Bhavnesh and Lalit," said Rita Sharma (62), a retired government official who lives right opposite the house of the Chundawat family.

When her house was being constructed in 1991, Ms. Sharma recalled, "They [Bhopal Singh and Narayan Devi] used to supervise the workers and even provided them water and tea at regular intervals."

The couple even took care of Ms. Sharma's one-year-old son Arnav when the Sharmas moved into their house in 1992. "From changing Arnav's nappies to feeding him to making him sleep, they took charge. He practically stayed with them in the initial years," she said.

Ms. Sharma said she never had to make pickle in the last 26 years because "Mummy" always had ready stock.

In 1993, Bhavnesh, his wife Savita and little Neetu came to Delhi from Rajasthan after Bhopal Singh summoned both his sons home. "I did not go because I met with an accident in 1992 and was on bed for about 12 months. My work in Rajasthan was also prospering," Mr. Dinesh said.

In the mid-1990s, Bhopal Singh's daughter Pratibha also came to stay with him in Delhi. Ms. Sharma claimed that Pratibha's husband Harinder Bhatia was an alcoholic and his family "did not treat her well".

"After Pratibha's husband's death, we did not think she would be happy at his house. Our father told us to bring her back, provide the best education to Priyanka [Pratibha and Harinder's daughter] and make her a successful individual," Mr. Dinesh said.

The family ran a grocery shop and plywood business in the area.

The family consisted of

Narayani Devi (80), mother of Bhuvnesh, Lalit and Pratibha

- Pratibha Bhatia (57), widowed daughter of Narayani Devi

- Bhuvnesh (50), elder son of Narayani Devi

- Lalit (45), younger son of Narayani Devi

- Savita (48), elder daughter-in-law of Narayani Devi, wife of Bhuvnesh

- Tina (42), younger daughter-in-law of Narayani Devi, wife of Lalit

- Priyanka (33), daughter of Pratibha

- Nitu (25), elder daughter of Bhuvnesh

- Monu (called "Menaka") (23), younger daughter of Bhuvnesh

- Dhruv (called "Dushyant") (15), only son and youngest child of Bhuvnesh

- Shivam (15), son and only child of Lalit.

In 2007 Lalit Chundawat's father Bhopal Singh died of natural causes. After the death of their father, Lalit became very introverted. One day, he told his family that he was possessed by his father's soul, who advised him the ways to attain a good life. Since 2007 he had been maintaining a diary on his father's "instructions".

Lalit's challenges

Lalit, who is at the centre of the macabre tragedy, was a rather complex character. Called kaka (uncle) by youngsters, he was funny, reserved, responsible, authoritative, all at once. He was also the only earning member when the Chundawat family moved to Delhi.

Chander Prakash Mehta, a resident of Tohana and Lalit's best friend since 1989, recalled that his friend was no stranger to challenges. Both of them studied medicine at a private college in Hisar.

"Lalit was a year senior in Inter College but he could not take exams in the junior year because he met with an accident. He had to repeat the year. In the senior year, during examinations, he fell ill again. He had to drop out," said Mr. Mehta.

After Lalit moved to Delhi, the two remained close friends, visiting each other regularly. Mr. Mehta remembered sitting for hours into the night with Lalit and talking about their friends from college. "Lalit joked a lot. He was probably the funniest in our group. But he was a no-nonsense man and he never compromised on principles."

Lalit started working at a plywood shop in Shahdara in the mid- 1990s and around 10 years ago, he opened his own shop in Burari. In February 2002, he got married to Tina. Three years later, their son Shivam was born.

In 2004, a major incident shook Lalit's life.

"He was pushed under several sheets of plywood and set on fire. We knew who did it but the matter was resolved through a compromise," said Mr. Dinesh. Lalit lost his voice in the incident.

Things began to change in Lalit's life in February 2007 after his father died of respiratory illness.

The death that changed it all

The whole family was devastated and a priest was called for Garuda Purana paath (a prayer) for 10 days after the death.

"One of those 10 days, we were all sitting and listening to the prayers when Lalit suddenly started chanting Om. His voice came back and everybody said 'Daddy aa gaye' [Daddy has returned]," she said.

This was perhaps the beginning of the end, said the neighbours.

Naresh Yadav, who lives a few houses away and was a regular customer at Lalit's shop, recalled a conversation with him in 2008. "I asked him how he regained his voice and he said his father came in his dream and asked him to perform a puja," he said, adding that Lalit never mentioned such dreams about his father again.

Ms. Sharma said Lalit and Bhavnesh's children used to call her for kirtans, which started soon after Bhopal Singh's death. "Every night around 9 p.m., they would sit together and pray for 15-30 minutes. The kids used to tell me 'Daddy ke aane ka time ho gaya' [it is time for grandfather to come]," she said.

During the kirtans , Lalit used to sit in front. Over the years he had taken the place of Bhopal Singh in the family.

Lifestyle changes

The Chundawats also adopted a lot of lifestyle changes. They stopped eating and cooking non-vegetarian food. Bhavnesh stopped drinking at home. The pujas became a regular affair. The number of shops increased from one to three, Lalit's plywood shop, Bhavnesh's grocery shop and the third one they were setting up together, so did the floors of the house.

The first mention of Bhopal Singh in Lalit's diaries is made on September 7, 2007, wherein the notes ask the family to keep his black and white photo in front of them and remember him. "Mann mein dhyan yahi rakho ki

Daddy meri purani aadatein chhut jaye [pray that you get rid of your old habits]," read the September note.

The diaries thereon are filled with instructions, in a strict, almost scolding tone, for all the family members to follow. They dictated the daily routine of the members, including their eating habits and other mundane activities, for financial and general betterment of the family. The notes appear to have a major bearing on the way all members of the family lived their lives.

Lalit's employee Ahmed Ali alias Pappu, who had been working with him for the last six years, said the man often brought his father into conversations. "He would mention uncle ji to show how one should be a good person," Ali said.

The week before the incident, Lalit was not going to his shop much. Ali said he was not keeping well and was spending most of the time sleeping at home.

Unable to wrap his head around the deaths and the alleged reason behind them, Ali said he always saw his employer as a kind and trustworthy person who went out of his way to help others.

"I was getting married in December 2016, a month after demonetization. Lalit bhaiyya used to stand in queues outside ATMs at 3 a.m. because I needed cash," he said as tears rolled down his eyes.

Close-knit family

Narayan Devi's daughters-in-law Savita and Tina fitted the stereotype of able homemakers. They woke up early, cooked for the family, took care of the children and elders, and were polite and well-behaved with everyone they met.

"Savita bhabhi did not seem very educated. Tina, on the other hand, was well-read and worldly, but both of them adhered to whatever Aunty ji [Narayan Devi] said," said Preet Kaur Mann, another neighbour who knew the Chundawat family for over 20 years.

Ms. Mann recalled the "thoughtful" nature of Savita and Tina with an anecdote. "A few months ago, the wife of one of their workers broke her leg. The Chundawats kept the woman at their house and both the bhabhis took care of her."

Easy-going' Bhavnesh

The elder son, Bhavnesh, was much more communicative than his younger brother, said Ms. Sharma. His grocery store was an 'adda' for people from all walks of life to come and chit-chat, and he would entertain them all with a warm smile.

Bhavnesh's daughter Neetu was a constant support for him as she used to sit with him at his shop and manage the finances. Her uncle Dinesh said she stood by her father like a rock.

The neighbours said that they were most shocked by Neetu's death. "She was a very confident and bubbly girl," said Amrik Singh Mann, Ms. Mann's husband.

She was the one who broke the news of the recent shootout in Burari to all the neighbours. "We do not understand how she got influenced into participating in such an exercise [the death]," said Mr. Mann.

Neetu had completed Class XII from DAV Public School and pursued her bachelors and masters degrees in commerce through correspondence.

Mr. Mehta said Neetu and her younger sister Maneka used to visit Tohana and stay at his house. Neetu was pursuing her masters from Lovely Professional University and the centre of her examination was near Tohana.

Maneka, on the other hand, was a quiet person for whom her studies mattered the most. She had completed her B.Sc from Delhi University and wanted to pursue masters in forensic science.

"Maneka did not open up to people much. She would go to her class, come back home and keep to her books mostly," recalled Ms. Sharma.

The lively teenagers

Like Maneka, Shivam and Dhruv too were bright students and always scored well in their exams. They were fond of motorbikes and cars, which the family did not possess.

Their friend Jatin recalled that the two followed a set routine and studied for at least two hours before going out to play at night. "We used to play cricket and go cycling almost every day. But for some reason they did not come to play in the last week of June," said the 15-year-old.

Jatin said both Dhruv and Shivam were extremely "god-fearing" for their age.

"On Sundays they used to worship the sun by offering water. Boys our age do not usually do that."

The two teenagers had no access to laptops and mobile phones, their friends said, adding that both of them could only use the computer at their house and that too under the surveillance of someone older.

"They were not allowed to use mobile phones. They would sometimes ask me for mine but Lalit bhaiyya had instructed me not to give it to them," Ali said.

Their uncle, Mr. Dinesh, remembered how the boys were fond of riding his two-wheeler. "We have learnt from mama [uncle], please let us ride it," they used to tell him.

A teacher at their school – Virendra Public School – said the boys were in the same class and had the same set of friends.

"They were extremely bright students and were also very active in extracurricular activities. They hardly missed school," he said.

The tutor at home

Jatin and his brother Aditya (11) were students of Pratibha. She used to take tuitions at home in the evening for students up to Class VIII.

"She was a tough teacher but a good one. She would scold us if we did not do our homework. She would also complain to our parents," said Jatin.

As for their part-time teacher Priyanka who used to teach them during her off days on weekends, Jatin and Aditya sang in chorus, "Pinku di was the best."

Priyanka, her neighbour Ms. Mann said, was a private person. She was not "loud" like her cousin Neetu, neither as quiet as Maneka. Priyanka was somewhere in the middle, who liked to live her life "in a controlled way".

Ms. Mann, who attended Priyanka's engagement on June 17, said the woman requested her not to post pictures on Facebook and tag her as she did not want people to know yet.

At CPA Global, where Priyanka was working since 2012, her seniors said, "She was exemplary at her work, and had won many trophies and certificates."

Her manager recalled that while she was cordial with everyone in office, she only had two-three friends who she used to interact with. "In fact, nobody at work knew that she was engaged. Only one of her friends was aware but even she was not invited," he said.

Priyanka used to participate in regular office events but "not the ones that stretched till late night", he added.

Not one of the family members gave Mr. Dinesh a hint of what was going on inside the Burari house. Though he is yet to come to terms with the tragedy, he said he could think of only one explanation for the secrecy. "They knew I did not believe in anything supernatural. They knew if they had told me, I would have stopped them at any cost."

Day of Incident

On 1st July 2018, when the neighbors, Gurcharan Singh, Kuldeep Singh, and Pritpal Kaur went to check the Bhatia family (originally Chundawat), who owned a grocery shop and had neither opened the same in the morning (which generally used to open at 5:30 am in the morning) nor had collected milk from the daily milk-man and were not responding to the neighbors' calls, they found the main door open as it was not locked from inside. As they went upstairs, they were left shocked to discover nine family members hanging from an iron grill on the ceiling of the roof in a circular formation. The tenth member, a lady, was hanging right opposite to them and their mother was lying in the other room, on the floor, near her bed. The family members were blindfolded, hands and feet bound, while they had hanged themselves. The family's dog, the only member alive, was tied on the roof and was said to be barking continuously.

Three generations lived together in the same house. All of the members were well-educated and well-adjusted social members. It was a family of 11 members who were living in that house in Burari, Delhi. The matriarch, Narayani Devi, was a widow who was a mother of three sons and two daughters, among which two sons and one daughter used to reside with her in that house. Bhuvnesh was the elder son and Lalit was the youngest. They were married to Savita and Tina respectively. While Bhuvnesh and Savita had two daughters and one son (Maneka, Neetu, and Dhruv), Lalit and Tina were parenting one son only, Shivam. Narayani Devi's daughter Pratibha was the mother of her only daughter Priyanka.

The family had a general store and the younger son, Lalit had a plywood business. Neighbors have claimed that the family was doing fairly well in both their businesses. Professed to be religious people, neighbors, relatives and associated colleagues claimed that the 11-member family involved nice, generous, and harmonious people who were never involved in fights amongst each other or with people around. While the children in the family were intelligent, good in academics, and offered respectful behaviour, the other members were eager to help their relatives and friends whenever in need. Sujata Nagpal, the surviving sister, and eldest brother, Dinesh, agreed to the opinions of the neighbors about her family when she was asked about the same. None of the family relatives were accepting the fact that the 11-member daily had attempted a mass suicide. This was majorly because the family had thrown a huge celebration for one of their daughters, Priyanka's engagement, that happened exactly 14 days before the occurrence of the discussed incident.

Discovery of bodies

On the morning of 1 July 2018 around 7:15 am, the neighbour Gurcharan Singh, who used to go on morning walks with one of the deceased, went to the Chundawat residence after noticing Lalit Chundawat's absence for the morning walk, as well as the fact that the Chundawat's shops were still not opened (the shops usually opened between 5 and 5:30 am). Gurcharan Singh found the door of the house open and the ten people, including Lalit Chundawat, hanging. He raised an alert by calling other neighbours, and police received the call around 7:30am

Ten of the eleven people – two men, six women and two teens – were found hanging in the courtyard of the house. They were blindfolded and their mouths were taped. Some of the bodies had their hands and feet tied as well. Another woman, 80-year-old Narayani Devi was found dead in another room. It appeared that she had been strangled.

Members of the family were found hanging from a mesh in their ceiling in the hallway, all close together. Their faces were wrapped almost entirely, ears plugged with cotton, mouths taped and hands tied behind the back. There were five stools, probably shared by the 10 members. Their faces were covered with cloth pieces cut from a single bed-sheet.

Tommy, the pet dog of the family, was the only survivor in the house. He was chained on the terrace and had a high fever when the police found him after discovering the 11 bodies. It was not clear who had tied him. He was later said to have been convalescing at Noida's House of Stray Animals, where he was taken immediately after being rescued.

Investigation

Evidence found in the house pointed to mass suicide for occult reasons, and Post-mortem examination of the bodies found no signs of struggle. Nevertheless, due to the public nature of the case, pressure from hardline groups, and accusations of a cover up from relatives, Police initially recorded the case as a murder and investigated the possibility of a murder motivated by non-occult reasons. Police found 11 diaries in the house, all of them maintained for the period of eleven years.

Joint Commissioner of Police (Crime) Alok Kumar stated: "We have found handwritten notes detailing how hands and legs are to be tied and are quite similar to the manner in which the bodies of 10 persons were found. They are exhaustive notes and we are studying them." Details written in the diaries match how the bodies were found with their faces covered, mouths taped, and cotton balls in ears. The bodies were discovered hanged in batches of three, which is what the diaries also state. The diary stated that the Bebe (elderly woman) could not stand and hence should be lying on the bed, which was consistent with the discovery of her being found strangled on the bed. The diary also mentions: "everyone will tie their own hands and when the kriya (ritual) is done then everyone will help each other untie their hands", indicating that the family was not expecting to die. Role of Lalit

Handwriting analysis revealed that these diaries were written by Priyanka (daughter of Pratibha) and Nitu (elder daughter of Bhuvnesh), but were supposedly dictated to Lalit by his late father's spirit. Lalit is believed to have masterminded the incident. The crime branch believes that Lalit and his wife Tina were responsible for tying the hands and legs of the family members. Lalit had told the family members that the soul of the husband of Narayani Devi had entered his body in order to get the family to follow him.

Crime branch and the investigation that was carried out

When the crime branch took into account every minute detailing in the house where the incident had taken place, they were of the opinion concerning a few things which were:

1.   The elder son, Bhuvnesh had tried to set his hands, which were tied, free, as clear signs of struggle could be seen in his fingers.

2.   The children of the house were tied not only by their hands but also by their feet, ruthlessly with telephone wires. There were no signs of struggle by any of them. Both eyes and mouths were taped and their ears were stuffed with cotton.

3.   The eldest member of the family, Narayani Devi was found lying dead in the other room beside her bed with a half-turned body. There was a belt around her neck which resulted in a few marks on the side of her neck.

4.   Everyone in the family had a scarf around their neck, which was used to hang themselves.

5.   Evidence of a ritual that was performed the night before was discovered as well. A leftover ritual pyre was found. From the ashes that were lying around the pyre, it was clear that the same was used a day prior to the incident.

6.   On 28th June 2018 (as the CCTV camera had shown), Tina, Lalit's wife, and her son, Shivam were seen to have purchased four stools. Further, on 30th June 2018 at 9:40 pm, Tina was seen to be carrying some newly purchased tools with Neetu. At 10:29 pm, Lalit's son, Shivam, was seen opening their plywood shop and carrying a small bundle of wires upstairs.

7.   A packet of milk was kept in the fridge for the following day's usage, and Lalit, the family's youngest son, had recharged the phones of other family members the day before the event. In the kitchen, soaked chana dal (black gram) was discovered, most likely for the next day's supper.

8.   A register was found beside the temple in the house. After a rigorous search, 11 diaries were discovered where the earliest entry was dated 2007 and the last entry was made the night before the incident (2018).

11 diaries and the story behind them

1.   The crime branch had opined that the language that was used in the diaries was instructional, commanding, and conversational. The last page of the diary had all the instructions that needed to be followed by the family, and that eventually unfolded to become a horrifying incident.

2.   The first mention of Bhopal Singh in Lalit's diaries occurs on September 7, 2007, when the notes had asked the family to remember

him by keeping his black-and-white photograph in front of them. The September message had stated, "Mann mein dhyan yahi rakho ki Daddy meri purani aadatein chhut jaye" [pray that you get rid of your old habits].

3.   On 24th June 2018, the last diary entry that was made explained a ritual called "Banyan Tree Ritual" which would run for a period of seven days along with the puja called, Badh Puja. Badh is originally a tree that has its roots hanging from the branches. The time of the incident was mentioned in the diary (supposedly at 1 am in the morning).

4.   Concerning the Badh Puja, it was instructed that;

1.   The same would be religiously carried out for a period of seven days and if anybody would have come to visit the family then the puja was supposed to take place the following day.

2.   It was directed that nothing related to the puja should be visible to any of the outsiders coming to the house.

3.   Dim light should be used in the puja and eyes should be completely shut.

4.   The blindfold should be properly tied in the eyes, the mouth should be gagged by a handkerchief, and the mind should be focused and empty. The eldest member, Narayani Devi was directed to complete the ritual by lying down only as she was aged and overweight.

5.   It was directed that while performing the puja, it should be imagined that the branches of the tree were wrapping themselves around an individual's body. The ritual should therefore be performed with unity and determination, which will help reduce mistakes.

4. The diaries mentioned every little and minute detail that the family was abiding by in order to conduct their lives. The diaries also had indications of the family conducting witchcraft and occult practices. It felt as if some third person or mystical energy was directing the 11 members thereby controlling them.

5. Although the crime branch had tried to contact some person with a religious or a spiritual background who were related to the family, their efforts went down the drain as no such contact was available.

Expert evidence and sayings in light of the Burari deaths case

The Bhatia family was headed by Bhopal Singh, the husband of Narayani Devi who had died in 2007. After his dismissal, the family was left with no one who could control it or be an authoritative figure to control the ups and downs associated with it. Clinical hypnotherapist Anita Anand claimed that in a typical Indian family when the patriarch dies, there is a vacuum in the family. A somewhat similar kind of incident could be noticed in this case. Bhopal Singh, until his death, used to control the family, their planning, children's education, etc. The responsibilities that Bhopal Singh used to swiftly carry out-landed over on his youngest son, Lalit's shoulders, after his death. Friends and relatives of Lalit voiced that it was because of his maturity and decision-making skills which made other family members follow him and treat his sayings as the supreme one. It is to be noted that neighbours, friends, and relatives of the family have repeatedly agreed to the fact that the deceased Bhopal Singh was a very nice, broad-minded human being and therefore it was unlikely of him expressing such commands.

Entry in the diary had started right after Bhopal Singh's death and the majority of the directions and diary entries were concerning Lalit. As the investigation proceeded, experts and state actors came to recognize the youngest son of Narayani Devi, Lalit to be the mind behind the Burari incident. Lalit was supposedly involved in direct communication with his deceased father in his dreams where his father used to tell him how to conduct the family and the same was followed. He started sharing these conversations with his family. It was Neetu, one of the children who had informed the neighbors that her uncle, Lalit, was possessed by their grandfather's spirit and it was the latter that guided them. Whenever Lalit used to converse with his family about the instructions he received from his dead father, his voice used to change to that of his father's. The diary clearly mentioned that the deceased father's spirit would visit the family every Tuesday, Thursday, Saturday, and Sunday. The instructions that were given resulted in the financial well-being of the family. This made the family believe more whatever the deceased father was directing. It was promised that the deceased father, Bhopal Singh was supposed to visit the family after completion of the Banyan Tree ritual and save the family members. The irony was although the family was made to believe that they will be saved, they eventually called their death all by themselves.

Savita and Tina, Narayani Devi's daughters-in-law, fulfilled the stereotype of capable housewives. They got up early, prepared food for the family, looked after the youngsters and the elderly and were kind and well-behaved to everyone they encountered.

Dr. Virendra Singh, Handwriting Division, Forensics Science Lab, Delhi was provided with the copies and diaries that were discovered from the Bhatia family's house for identifying the handwriting in the entries. It was revealed that Pratibha's daughter, Priyanka, and Bhuvnesh's daughter, Neetu, were the ones who were writing these notes.

As it slowly came out to the experts involved in the present case that Lalit was the one behind the incident, they could gradually read the minds of Lalit and the thought-process he had been going through. In many ways, he had felt being out of control, as has been explained by clinical hypnotherapist Anita Anand.

The Chundawats changed their way of life as well. They ceased to consume and prepare non-vegetarian meals. At home, Bhavnesh quit drinking. Pujas became a common occurrence. The number of stores expanded from one to three, including Lalit's plywood shop, Bhavnesh's grocery store, and the third one they were opening jointly, as well as the house's floors.

The story surrounding Lalit

1.   In 1988, Lalit had his first bike accident because of which he was hospitalized for a prolonged period. It was revealed that due to the accident, Lalit had suffered head injuries. Friends have claimed that he used to fall asleep very early.

2.   After shifting to Delhi, Lalit had been subjected to another attack on 26th March 2004, which was more about an attack with an intention to kill him. This incident had taken place when Lalit used to work in a plywood shop in the suburbs across the Yamuna river. He was locked in the shop and set ablaze. This occurrence had resulted in Lalit losing his voice. Vascular surgeon, Dr. Ambrarish Satwik observed that it was highly unlikely for a person to lose his voice unless there is physical damage, trauma, or disease in the larynx.

3.   Clinical psychologist, Dr. Roma Kumar made an observation in light of the present case stating that nobody in the family had tried to offer treatment for helping Lalit recover from Post-Traumatic Stress Disorder (PTSD). Although the doctor who had treated Lalit had suggested

a psychiatrist check-up taking into notice his conditions, the family had ignored the same.

4.   In the language of psychology, if a trauma is not treated in any individual who has been subjected to it, a certain level of psychosis sets in, which is the inability of the mind to deal in a rational way. One of the direct results of psychosis is hearing voices. A year after his father's death, Lalit had regained his voice.

5.   Neighbors have claimed that Lalit's behaviour pattern appeared to be changing a few days before Priyanka's engagement was scheduled to take place. It was possibly his belief system that reminded him that nobody should be leaving the house and going away. He had slept for a period of two days at a stretch after the engagement.

6.

Conclusion

It is said that one of the things that had gone clearly wrong with this case and the reason why people have very little knowledge about the Burari case was because of the way it was reported, possibly in a crime drama manner. The involvement of numerology and 'tantrik' dimensions have been key catalysts in presenting the case in an exaggerated way before the general public. The Burari incident speaks of the lack of interconnectedness in society. To a considerable extent, Indian culture is clearly unprepared to address mental health difficulties in ways other than appealing to morals or repeating religious precepts. It exacerbates the challenges caused by society's rapid change. Ancient community relationships are still important to many individuals, but they are disintegrating in many circumstances, not only because traditional standards no longer match a modernizing society. This is most visible in cities, but it also impacts rural communities, which now have access to not just mass media and the internet, but also connect with relatives who have relocated to the metropolis. India's mental-health system must become an essential element of the country's overall healthcare structure if it is to develop. Psychiatrists and psychologists must work more closely with general practitioners and specialists.

The Alavander Murder Case 1952

INTRODUCTION

In 1995 the name of the city of Bombay was changed to Mumbai and a year in 1996 the name of the city of Madras was changed to Chennai. This incident happened way back in the 1950's, so I will refer to both cities as Bombay and Madras as that Is what they were known as when this crime occured.

BACKGROUND:

Alavandar lived in Madras during World war II, He had worked as a sub-divisional officer at the army head quarter in Avadi, and when the war ended he found employment selling pens, in a very popular and very respectful shop named 'German company'. He proved to be a very good salesperson- he was charming and helpful and would always appear very smartly dressed, as though he liked his job very much.

He wanted to work for himself and have his own business- now in his early 40's the opportunity arose for him to set up a small company where he could sell small plastic goods, these colourful items were expensive and attracted a lot of attention from curious shoppers in early 1950's in Madras.

He had been fortunate enough as he had been given permission to set up his store in front of the much larger German company shop, where he had previously worked as a salesman. That location was good, as German company had a well-established business, all the customers had to cross ALavander store in order to enter German company shop, and because of Alavender's friendly and persuasive nature ,his business prospered as his store dealt in of household plastic items, it was mainly women that looked around and purchased his goods. Having such a large female customer base, he decided to sell sarees as well with others items; this proved to be very a very wise decision.

Many ladies came to his store and his business started to grow, however he hadn't enough money to pay the installments. Despite the fact he was married with two children, Alavanadar would allow the women a payment break in exchange for certain sexuaL favours. In the summer of 1951, a young lady named Devaki came to the store; she was originally from Kerala and now lived with her parents in Madras. Alavannder wasted no time in using his charm to try and seduce her and by October of the same year they would meet at a local hotel. When she realized that he was married, Devaki broke up the relationship in May 1952.

She met an insurance clerk named Prabhakar Menon and the following month they got married and now focused on her future, she thought she could put her past and Alavender behind her and along with her husband she moved to a rented property in the Royalpuram district of Madras. Here they were able to employ a boy to assist with cooking and cleaning. Everything seemed to be going well for the couple. Prabhakar was earning more money as he changed employments to a better paid position at the freedom newspaper, the newspaper generated much of its revenue through companies that placed advertisements.

It was in a small plastic store ran by Alavender that Prabhakar met with Alavender to discuss the possibility of increasing the size of his adverts, Alavander offered Prabhakar his congratulations on marrying such a beautiful lady, Prabhakar considered it strange that someone was talking about the woman he had recently married and wondered exactly how well the store owner and his wife actually knew each other.

Thereafter he questioned Devaki who denied that she had ever had a relationship with Alavender, but Prabhakar sensed that she seemed anxious and uneasy about answering his questions, over the following weeks he continued to question her until towards the end of the August ......

Devaki who was by now exasperated by her husband's continued questioning, told him the truth and explained that she once had a relationship with Alavender before she and Prabhakar knew each other; she then told him that before Prabhakar, there were two men. Alavender had contacted her saying that he would not place advertisements in a newspaper unless she renewed their relationship,

Prabhakar was beside himself with rage- How dare of a store owner disrespect him and his wife.

THE CRIME: how they murdered Alavender

On august 28th when Mrs. Alavender went to sleep , her husband had not come home from work but she presumed he was out with the other business owner and would return around midnight; however when she awoke on 29th of August he was still not back. Somewhat worried, she went to his business place, she asked the other store owners and soon discovered that he had gone off with a woman shortly after 12:00 p.m.

But he had said that he would return to the store within a couple of hours no one however had seen or heard from him, then the staff for the pen company told her that her husband left the shop on the previous day around noon with a woman who came to meet him and he told them that he was going to Royalpuram; she was told that the woman he had left with was from Kerala and lived at 62 Cemetery road in the Royalpuram district.

She went to the house and knockedthe door; it was answered by Prabhakar who told her that he had not seen her husband and he did not have any reason to come to his house; by now she was getting worried about her husband as he had never just disappeared before, she returned to the store where she saw the owner of German company who told her that she should go to the police and he agreed to accompany her to the station where Mrs. Allavander registered his missing report.

In 1952 Madras was a large city with a population of 1.5 million people so where Alavander had disappeared, was not so difficult task but he had a stall, a wife and children and this was totally out of character for him so, the police took the statement from Mrs. Alavander very seriously. 500 kms away in Madurai the passengers in the third class carriage of the Indo salon express train that had left Madras at 8:00 the previous day, alerted the guard that there was a green trunk under the one of the seats from which was emanating a terrible smell.

The train was halted at the station and the police was called to investigate. When they opened the trunk they discovered the decapitated human body the humidity and the heat had accelerated the rate of decomposing so the police wasted no time in taking the trunk to the cowry, so a post-mortem could be performed; the pathologist observed that there were stab wounds to the chest which could have been the cause of death, that there was however nothing found in the trunk that could help identify the deceased. When the inspector at the Esplanade Police station of Madras learned that a headless corpse was found on a train that had left the city a few hours after Alavander had last been seen, he wondered if it was possible that it could be 'the missing' man.

The investigation into finding Alavander was led by inspector Amin Allen who sent one of his constables to the house at 62 Cemetery road where it was reported the woman last seen with Alavender lived, but when the constable arrived there was no one home; he spoke to the neighbors who said that the family had left the house and they believed that they may have gone to Bombay.

Inspector Raman Arden arrived and entered the property. There were traces of blood, the inspector then asked the local people if they had seen anything suspicious, the next day a policeman on his daily round saw an object floating in the bay, he went to the seashore, reached out to look at what it was, it was wrapped in a brown shirt; he managed to pull it to the shore and when he looked closer he was shocked he discover that it was a human head.

Finding the head in Madras and finding a headless body on a train that started its journey in Madras led inspector Raman Aden to conclude that in all probability, the head belonged to the body which he believed was that of the missing Alavander.

The body was transported to Madras where a second post-mortem was carried out, the results of which confirmed the inspector's suspicions that the head and the body were of the same person; fingerprints were taken and they matched those from Alavander's military records, Mrs. Alavander also confirmed that the deceased was her husband. The police now had the identity of the victim but they did not have the person or people who were responsible for the crime. They needed to speak to Prabhakar and Devaki.

Inspector Raman hadn travelled to Bombay and with the assistance of the Bombay police managed to trace the suspects who were staying in the home of one of Prabhakar's relatives; they went to the house and arrested them before escorting them back to Madras. While the inspector was in Bombay, his police team had been gathering evidence. Other important items were found, including the knife that he had used to commit the terrible crime. They also spoke to the owner of the store where the knife had been purchased who confirmed that it was bought by a man on 28th of August and the man looked very much like Prabhakar..

The police also interviewed the accused couples' 13 year old servant boy who told them that he had heard Prabhakar and Devaki talk about a man.

He also said that he heard Prabhakar telling his wife to get him back to the house where they could rid themselves of him, he also said that that when her husband was at work, Devaki would sometimes go her room and cry, On the 28th of August, Prabhakar had given him some money and told him not to return until after dark, he said that when he did he looked solemn and was washing some clothes. He asked if he could help but she told him that she would do it herself. The police also managed to find a faintly blood stained saree which they presumeDevaki had worn on the day of the murder. In the house, a palm print was visible on the kitchen wall and tests proved that it was the palm of Prabhakar. Blood was also found under a stone grinder. Slowly the inspector was piecing together the events of August 28th 1952- everything pointed to Prabhakar and Devaki being the killers but there were no eyewitnesses and the inspector could not be completely certain exactly how the events had unfolded that night in order to secure a conviction. He offered Devaki a deal- in exchange for a pull pardon she would give evidence against Prabhakar.   Devaki however was not interested in a deal; she remained completely loyal to her husband.

THE TRIAL:

The story had filled with newspapers and intrigued the public so when the trial began at the Madras High Courts the courtroom was full and large crowds gathered outside. Prabhakar and and Devaki Menon both pleaded not guilty to all charges. The prosecution told the courts that this was a planned and premeditated murder- the husband doing away with his wife's lover. They called many witnesses and built up a very strong case against the accused- The store owner who sold the knife used in the crime, confirmed that he sold it to the male defendant on the morning of the 28th August and the servant boy confirmed he had been sent out all day and told not to come back until midnight. Staff at Chairman Company told the court that Devaki had visited Allivander Store that day and Allivander then went off to her house shortly afterwards.

The scene at Madras High Court —

To avoid losing the accused at Madras High Court, they were locked behind a concealed door on the floor at the 4th Court hall. After every hearing, they were sent back in and the hall was armed with strict security

.The police had also found out more evidence to make the case stronger — Devaki's blood-stained saree from the murder scene that she had thrown in a park at Broadway. A knife which is commonly known as Malabar knife was also recovered adding more evidence to the murder. Even the shop where Devaki's husband had brought the knife from, was traced out.

The defense lawyer argued that such a murder was committed for the purpose of self-defense as Alavandar had continually disturbed Devaki even after marriage. In response to this statement, the learned state prosecutor argued that self-defense must include two important elements, first is that there should have been an imminent threat or danger to one's personal safety or property and second is that the force used for the purpose of self-defense must be a force that is enough to stop the other person from attacking. This case cannot amount to self-defense due to the lack of these two elements and it was further argued that the murder was a pre-planned one.

The trial was presided by Justice A.S.P. Iyer. The learned state prosecutor built up a strong case of a pre-planned heinous murder. Justice A.S.P. Iyer sentenced Devaki's husband to 7 years of imprisonment and 3 years of imprisonment to Devaki.

After serving in Prison —

After getting released from prison, Devaki and her husband set up a tea shop in Kerala. Over the years they prospered and turned their small tea shop into a big hotel.

THE END

Printed in the USA
CPSIA information can be obtained
at www.ICGtesting.com
CBHW031520081024
15567CB00044B/316